Jorge Luis Borges

Titles in the series Critical Lives present the work of leading cultural figures of the modern period. Each book explores the life of the artist, writer, philosopher or architect in question and relates it to their major works.

In the same series

Jean Genet
Stephen Barber

Michel Foucault
David Macey

Pablo Picasso
Mary Ann Caws

Franz Kafka
Sander L. Gilman

Guy Debord
Andy Merrifield

Marcel Duchamp
Caroline Cros

Frank Lloyd Wright
Robert McCarter

James Joyce
Andrew Gibson

Jean-Paul Sartre
Andy Leak

Noam Chomsky
Wolfgang B. Sperlich

Jorge Luis Borges

24 August 1899 p 20
14 June 1986 p 142

Jason Wilson

REAKTION BOOKS

To Andrea

Published by Reaktion Books Ltd
33 Great Sutton Street
London EC1V ODX, UK

www.reaktionbooks.co.uk

First published 2006

Printed and bound in Great Britain
by Cromwell Press, Trowbridge, Wiltshire

British Library Cataloguing in Publication Data
Wilson, Jason, 1944–
    Jorge Luis Borges. – (Critical lives)
    1. Borges, Jorge Luis, 1899–1986 2. Authors, Argentine – 20th
    century – Biography
    I.Title
    868.6'209

    ISBN-13: 978 1 86189 286 7
    ISBN-10: 1 86189 286 1

Contents

Jorge Luis Borges in Paris in 1983.

Introduction

I met Borges briefly and formally several times; I heard him
give his idiosyncratic talks in London, Boston and Buenos Aires.
I have written on him as a literary critic and drafted the anonymous obituary for *The Times*.[1] Reading Borges was sufficient, the
real thrill. The Mexican novelist Carlos Fuentes discovered Borges
as a teenager while his father was posted as a diplomat in Buenos
Aires in the 1940s, and decided that he never wanted to meet
Borges, though reading him changed his life.[2] The problem with
any biography of Borges is that his outer life was dull and regular;
he was not a man of action and adventures. No Rimbaud, not a
Hemingway. He read voraciously and omnivorously, far more
than his readers, and a biography of the mind of a reader like
Borges would parody his own writings. Yet, there have been
numerous biographies of Jorge Luis Borges. My intention is not
to rehash this research but to see how biography illuminates the
work of this self-effacing man. One way into his life and mind will
be through his literary friends. I begin with Victoria Ocampo's
off-the-cuff comment that Jorge Luis Borges did not deserve the
talent he had. There's a flaw, she hints, between his staggering
intelligence, his wit and his behaviour.[3] When she founded her
cosmopolitan literary journal *Sur* in 1931 it opened with an essay
by Borges in the first issue. He was her star local writer. One of
her lovers, the French writer Pierre Drieu La Rochelle, remarked
in 1933 that the long journey to Buenos Aires was worth it just to

chat with Borges, and he had yet to write the stories that would make him famous.

I shall constantly insist on the sheer quirkiness and opacity of Borges. An Argentine critic recently grumbled that foreigners tended to view Borges as a kind of ET, an adorable alien, but that too has its grain of truth.[4] In one of his most memorable parables called 'Borges and I', first published in a magazine when blind in 1957, we see Borges's self as divided, but not in any Jekyll-and-Hyde sense, with a darker side (despite Borges's adoration of Stevenson). What I take from this parable is the idea that he has no fixed self, often dramatizing an ironic version of himself in his own stories. Borges wrote a book on Buddhism with Alicia Jurado in 1976, was a constant reader of Schopenhauer and was genuinely modest, a joker who belittled himself with almost a Buddhist giggle.

The psychology of a reader is strange. Who are you when you're reading about somebody else? That vicarious experience behind reading suggests a quality in Borges, the arch-reader. Borges posited that when we read a line by Shakespeare, we become Shakespeare, and when we read Dostoevsky's *Crime and Punishment* we become Raskolnikov. That is, as a reader we are invaded by the author, or, put another way, we are released from being our known selves. In a footnote to the fantasy story 'Tlön, Uqbar, Orbis Tertius', written in 1940 and collected as the opening 'story' of *Ficciones* (1944), we read that one of the churches in the ideal world of Tlön preaches that all men in the vertiginous moment of copulation are the same man. This sexual act, strangely absent in his fictions, strips us of our societal masks, our personalities, and we become Adam and Eve again. So anyone who repeats a line from Shakespeare is Shakespeare and Shakespeare is nobody.[5] Shakespeare becomes the experience of reading literature itself. In 1933 Borges postulated (one of his favourite philosophical verbs like 'refute') that 'no one is substantially someone: anyone can be anyone else, at any moment of time'. In 1941 he repeated this provocative notion that 'no man knows who he is, no man is somebody'[6] about the film *Citizen Kane* (Borges was a film critic in the 1940s). This odd statement, counter to our belief in a solid self, emerges from reading, which is a casting off of false selves and a fictive adopting of an alien or alter-self that lasts the act of reading itself, as short or long as it may be. In reading and copulating we melt into our deeper, anonymous selves where we are all the same. Was Borges joking? Did he believe this Platonic process? My questions show, already, how hard it is to read Borges's writing biographically. He was a teaser. You could easily refute his provocation that reading and copulation are similar acts based on self-forgetting.

How quickly – within a sentence – one character becomes his opposite, his double, is not based on psychology, but on how a reader becomes a character. The story 'The Theologians' ends in heaven, where God couldn't care less about the theological squabbles and confuses Aurelian with his enemy John of Pannonia. We read: 'It is more correct to say that in paradise, Aurelian discovered that in the eyes of the unfathomable deity, he and John of Pannonia (the orthodox and the heretic, the abominator and the abominated, the accuser and the victim) were a single person.'[7] Underneath our apparent differences we are archetypes, one person, nobody. Borges often cited Paul Valéry (more as thinker than poet) that all literature is written by one pluri-named person, the human spirit. My guess is that Borges turns all literature into what a reader does with a text, and readers are usually anonymous. Both writers and readers vanish into words, which resist individuality and particularity to leave us with the essential Platonism of language. That language writes us and discards our uniqueness was Borges's wager against the literary ego.

I return to the idea of two 'Borgeses' of his parable about the self 'Borges and I' in *El hacedor* ('The Maker') of 1960. One of the two selves is the famous one, who dazzled the world's leading intellectuals and writers from John Updike to George Steiner, Octavio Paz to

Michel Foucault. This Borges is the creation of his work, the 'Borges' in the minds of his readers, who know nothing about the 'real' fleshy, domestic Borges. This celebrated writer shared the Prix Formentor in 1961 with Samuel Beckett, though notoriously and disgracefully never the Noble Prize (in the same boat as Nabokov and Joyce). This other Borges is now the canonical writer in encyclopaedias and histories of literature. 'The greatest writer in Spanish since Góngora', the Cuban writer Guillermo Cabrera Infante once wrote. This celebrated Borges is vain, takes over. He has become a Monument. The humble Borges doesn't recognize himself in this other man. This man was once asked in the street if he was Borges, and he answered 'sometimes'. Both selves share a passion for faking and exaggerating; both passed through phases of writing about the outskirts of Buenos Aires and then elaborated games about time and infinity, but the main point is that their relationship is *hostile*. The modest Borges wants to escape his fame, runs away, likes strolling through Buenos Aires or studying maps or tasting coffee, the simple things of life (Borges was always ascetic and frugal). The other one is constantly stopped in the streets with his blindman's cane, congratulated on simply being Borges, a beloved national icon on postage stamps and in tourist brochures. Borges ends his parable about warring selves with a conundrum about creativity: 'I don't know who of the two writes this page.' He is both. Many times Borges looked back on an earlier self as alien; he almost accepts his own biography as a series of monads, self-sufficient, unrecognizable selves. In a note in 1941 Borges asserts his understanding of multiple selves in time: 'Like all men, Rudyard Kipling was many men', and Borges lists them.[8] There are many Borgeses; he didn't like being himself. A poem to Emerson, one of his literary mentors, ends: 'My name walks all over the continent; / I have not lived. I want to be someone else.'[9] Was he jesting? Biography must assimilate Borges's own experiences as a reader. He claimed that when we read Poe we contact a

'Poe' not only in each sentence that we read by him, but also the 'writer' of the sentences as an image of somebody greater than the text itself. The biographical Poe is not identical to the 'Poe' we create in our reader's mind as we read, whom we get to know and recognize so well. So with Borges.

El hacedor (1960), a miscellany of short prose pieces and poems, was his first book of new poems since 1929. (I'll be returning to this writer's block of 31 years, though he did add some new poems to his *Poemas 1922–1943*, which hardly counts as a new book.) In the epilogue, Borges, now blind, summarizes his 61 years of life. 'Few things have happened to me, though many things I have read.'[10] Years later, he corrected this lapidary phrase: 'As I've read a lot, many things have happened.'[11] So, the best things that have happened to him were reading Schopenhauer and learning the verbal music of England.[12] This 61-year-old's insight leads to a parable about solipsism; a man decides to draw the world. After years of filling in kingdoms, mountains, bays, horses and people and, just before dying, he realizes that his 'patient labyrinth of lines' has traced the image of his own face. Here is a clue to the man Borges. You can only know your contingent self in time, but you cannot know the objective, empirical world. The world you think you are getting to know is a projection of your own enigma. Here is a meditative man for whom the outside, the objective world, matter little. For example, he never read newspapers, claiming they were written to be forgotten the following day. He loathed mirrors, procreation, his own body and continually dreamt of labyrinths, masks and mirrors. That quality of self-dislike is the inner war anatomized in 'Borges and I'. Years later, in 1972, Borges wrote a poem about this inner strife called 'El centinela' ('The Sentry') where the other Borges imposes his memory, his lovelessness, his cult of ancestors and courage. Borges feels like the *enfermero* (nurse) of the other one in his steps, in his voice. The key line, repeated later as we'll note, is 'Minuciosamente lo odio' ('I hate him meticulously').[13] He loathes his other self in every minute detail.

Even if he were to commit suicide, there would still be another self: 'there I would be, waiting for myself'. In the end, then, Borges, as a reader, was reading himself. We learn about the divided man as we learn how and who he reads. Of course, if Borges is right, a biography is also about the biographer.

Borges summarized his life once again in 1974 in the epilogue to his two-volumed *Obras completas*, still the best edition in Spanish. This epilogue gives a wonderful image of the man. Claiming to be a note in the bogus *Enciclopedia Sudamericana*, published in Chile in 2074 (100 years into the future), it's a typical Borgesian faking of texts and dates, and further proof of his love for reading encyclo-paedias and maps. We learn that he was born in 1899, that his father was a lecturer in psychology, that he had a sister called Norah. He loved literature, philosophy and ethics. He thought that Cervantes could not have written *Don Quixote* and read few novels except for those by Voltaire, Stevenson, Conrad and Eça de Queiroz. He adored short stories, citing Poe's dictum about there being no such thing as a long poem. He taught at Harvard, got honorary degrees, but loathed bibliographies, the paraphernalia of scholarship. In 1960 he became a conservative. His fame led to countless critical studies. He admired valour. He wrote lyrics for some *milongas* (rural dance music), a biography of a minor local poet and tried to forge a new mythology for Buenos Aires as the city lacked one. He simplified Spanish, stripping it of its baroque armour thanks to his mentors Paul Groussac and Alfonso Reyes. He didn't believe in personality, citing Carlyle about history being a text we are forced to read and write and which writes us.[14] Later he would insist that Dante's *Divina Commedia* was written by many others, by the *espíritu humano*.[15]

Most of this self-obituary agrees factually with the obituary I wrote for *The Times*. What did he skip out? First, he doesn't mention his sister's husband Guillermo de Torre, the Spanish avant-garde poet and critic who broke into the closed family circle.

Then he avoids his love life, the string of non-consummated crushes. He always had, said Silvina Ocampo, an 'artichoke heart'. Third, no mention of his formidable, mass-going mother Leonor Acevedo, who kept Borges at home with her until she died aged 99 and even collaborated in translations of Kafka and Virginia Woolf with him. These are glaring gaps. But more amusingly, he dismissed those essay-cum-short-story-cum-book reviews that he baptized 'fictions' and that made him world-famous. Not one reference to this work of the 1940s, *Ficciones* or *El Aleph* (some 33 stories in all). Just that he read some novels, wrote poems, a quirky biography, and reshaped the numbed Spanish language. Borges once said that he was weary of his labyrinths.[16] Here, in his mock 1974 obituary, he appears fed up with what made him 'Borges'.

So I circle back to the flaw in Borges, his uncanny oddity, his utter quiddity. Before coming to his first 30 years, I want to stress one word from his wonderful essay 'The Argentine Writer and Tradition', a clever defence and inversion of Argentine provincialism and oceanic distance from Europe. We Argentines are free, he said, to read what we want when we want; we are not victims of a monolithic tradition. It's an attack on nationalism during Perón's authoritarian and fascist government. He gave this piece as a talk in the Colegio Libre de Estudios Superiores in 1950; someone had typed it and he added it, by backdating, to a new edition of his 1932 collection of essays *Discusión* ('Argument'). Borges constantly revised and excised his texts (and belittled chronology and facts). He forbade republication of his early essays – *Inquisiciones* in 1925, *El tamaño de mi esperanza* ('The Shape of my Hope') in 1926, *El idioma de los argentinos* ('The Language of the Argentines') in 1928 – though his widow María Kodama published them posthumously. But beyond the history of this influential talk, beyond its content, Borges identified Argentine culture as 'irreverent' in its relationship to Spain and Europe.[17] That word *irreverent* epitomizes Borges; there's an Imp of Perversion at play; you cannot pin him

p 56: July 1923 - one year

down, he's the Joker, the Trickster, a mischief-maker. He told an early French interviewer that he slips jokes (*blagues*) into his text.[18] He doesn't revere. Irreverence is an avant-garde dissonance at work in his thinking: I am nobody, I don't have a personality, we are nobodies underneath the surface personalities and so on. These are 'boutades' ('flashes of wit'); Borges assumed the avant-garde tactic of *épater le bourgeois* ('to shock the middle classes'), even though he was one himself, wore a buttoned-up suit, looked respectable and shockable, and drank milk everyday. This humorous streak surfaces brilliantly in his interviews, his sudden sentence endings, his unpredictable adjectives, his random lists, his contradictions, his sly comments and especially his mock erudition . . . it's a facet of his literary self. Norman Thomas di Giovanni, who worked with him for nearly five years, underlined that 'whim, caprice and daydreams guided him, even in his private life'.[19]

In 1922, aged 23 and after having lived fourteen crucial years in war-torn Europe, Borges articulated his anti-psychological version of what makes a person tick in his first essay back home in Buenos Aires titled 'La nadería de la personalidad' ('The Nothingness of Personality'), belittling the pre-eminence of the ego. No such thing as an ego, he wrote impishly. Every moment of life is complete and sufficient. Each moment you live abolishes all the past as it moves into the future. All that remains is episodic, circumstantial. We are nobodies. Later in 1942 he would write a fabulous story, 'Funes el memorioso' ('Funes, His Memory'), about a Uruguayan farm-worker with a perfect memory. This semi-literate Ireneo Funes was crippled after being thrown from a horse and then couldn't forget anything. Yet to remember the past in such precise detail he had to stop living the present, stop accumulating future memories. Borges's attack on the ego echoed T. S. Eliot's exploration of the poet's escape from personality as a relief from egomania. Borges tagged a literary label to what he loathed: the 'egolatría romántica'

14

('romantic ego-worship') and the 'vocinglero individualismo' ('vociferous individualism') that our societies still worship. Most interestingly, Borges acknowledged the influence of Buddhism in his thinking about himself.

Can we call Borges a Buddhist? Can his fascination with Buddhism tell us something about the man himself? My guess is that he was temperamentally a Buddhist, but also that he studied its philosophy and doctrine, one of his *aficiones* ('enthusiasms') listed in the 1979 epilogue to the second volume of his *Obras completas*. He discovered Buddhism in Geneva in 1914, through Schopenhauer, and remained a lifelong fan. In 1980 he confirmed that Buddhism reiterated what he had found in Hume and Macedonio Fernández. For example, Borges mocked theology and philosophy as being branches of fantastic literature, as having no truth value. He loved reading about systematic philosophy, but developed an anti-intellectual strain close to the Buddhist dismissal of pointless speculation. His sceptical attitude resembles Bertrand Russell's, an author, Borges once quipped, that he would take with him to a desert island. Borges worshipped logical absurdities, he told Fernando Sorrentino.[20]

In 1976 a blind Borges collaborated with an early biographer and friend, Alicia Jurado, to write *Qué es el budismo* ('What is Buddhism'). In a note, Alicia Jurado insists that the work is essentially Borges's, taken from his lecture notes at the Colegio Libre de Estudios. Without labouring the point, I can read many of Borges's traits back into Buddhism. For a start, Borges shared Buddhism's atheistic position, that it has not initiated a war, preaches tolerance, has no priests (just monks) and that it works to free the self from attachments.[21] The practice of the middle path is close to Borges's own life: no extremes of sensuality or of asceticism, no guilt, no repentance, no pardon, for all takes place in the mind, Buddhism's absolute idealism. Moderation was Borges's daily practice. Buddhism also negates history, for all the past resides in one mental space. Homer is all men, now, Borges wrote. This rubbishing of chronology, of facts, is notorious in Borges, who thinks along Jungian, archetypal lines. He was not interested in names and dates; all thinkers replay Plato and Aristotle, all writers are Homer or Shakespeare.[22] 'Descreo en la historia' ('I do not believe in history'), he wrote in 1942.[23] As he said about the Bengal poet Tagore and all Easterners, 'eternity interested them, and not time'. Borges would often shift perspectives from chronology to eternity in his stories in order to belittle human pretensions. This abrupt narrative shift is part of Borges's way of feeling: 'Let's imagine, *sub specie aeternitus*, a Droctulft', he wrote in 'Historia del rey y de la cautiva' ('Story of the Warrior and the Captive Maiden'), but not Droctulft as an individual who doubtless was unique and fathomless, like all individuals, 'but the generic type who is the work of oblivion and memory'.[24] We return to that generic essence thanks to this timeless angle.

Equally dismissed by Borges and Buddhism is the external world, objective reality. At a literary level, Borges mocks realism because he doesn't believe that language can grasp reality. In his parable about the absurdity of making sense of the world through books, 'The Library of Babel' (1941), the narrator turns to the reader and asks: 'You who read me, are you certain you understand my language?'[25] Buddhism also helps us understand Borges's laughing at erudition, his scorn for pedantry, for bibliographies, as he said. You cannot learn to become a Buddhist through books and ideas. It's a moral practice. Borges sees intellectual history as a history of pretension and absurdities. In his fantasy story narrated by the Minotaur, 'La casa de Asterión', we learn that 'like the philosopher, I think that nothing can be communicated by the art of writing'.[26] This may not be Borges speaking, but this idea about the limits of words surfaces throughout his work. Buddhism also warns that language cannot communicate Nirvana, the void beyond appearances. Truth is not found in words; Borges's greatest fable, the fiction 'The Aleph', is also a Buddhist joke. The vision granted to Borges under the staircase in the story cannot be recreated in sequential words, despite Borges's lists. Only a mystic outside time can see everything at once, but then cannot communicate it (Borges twice experienced a timeless moment). But most cogent in Borges's keen study of Buddhism is the negation of the self, of ego; its essential dogma. There is no self, just inner witnesses, spectators, 'Borges and I', always two Borgeses in bickering conflict.[27] In a comment on this piece, Borges described a reoccurring experience of his that what was happening to him was not happening to him. He traced his sudden sense of unreality back to one of the Indian schools of philosophy. Borges sought peace of mind, happiness or serenity, freedom from emotions, from sexual cravings, from fame, from his own intense bookishness. Negating the self and plunging into the inner void was a relief.[28] A delightful modesty was the consequence. According to Borges's take on Buddhism, each of us is an illusion vertiginously produced by a series of momentary and solitary versions of previous selves.[29] It's the theme of his fiction 'The Circular Ruins' which ends 'with relief, with humiliation, with terror, he realized that he too was but appearance, that another man was dreaming him'.[30] We are all hungry ghosts, without essential identity. Borges was not a practising Buddhist, but he did meditate on many Buddhist texts as a reader; he did convey that all his reading was a special kind of *attention*.

María Kodama, the closest person to Borges over the last decade of his life, told an interviewer that Borges had an Oriental way of feeling, derived from all that he had read in Buddhism.[31] As late as 1980 Borges reiterated that one of our of main delusions is the 'ego'. Borges's first biographer in English, Emir Rodríguez Monegal, noticed that Borges's theory of 'la nadería de la personalidad' ('the nothingness of personality') cuts across all his work. As early as 1923 on the flap of his first book of privately printed poems, *Fervor de Buenos Aires*, Borges wrote about the similarity between the writer and the reader: 'our nothings are little different; it's trivial and pure chance that you are the reader of these exercises and I their recorder'.[32] My point is that this is no theory, but a personality trait. Borges constantly mocked ego identity throughout his work. For example, in 'The Immortal' we read that 'no one is someone; a single immortal man is all men. Like Cornelius Agrippa, I am god, hero, philosopher, demon and world – which is a long-winded way of saying I am not.'[33] His greatest literary ambition, he wrote in 1945, was to write a book, a page, a paragraph, which is everything for all readers, and nothing to do with the actual Borges himself.[34]   *in "books" not bio -*

Alicia Jurado (b. 1922), who wrote biographies of Borges, W. H. Hudson and Cunninghame Graham, and was a novelist and naturalist, surveyed her lifelong friendship with Borges in the second volume of her memoirs, *El mundo de la palabra* (1990). She is a stern person, with a beautiful face, who lives in the flat Bioy Casares and Silvina Ocampo once lived in where Borges would eat and write almost every night on the corner of calle Ecuador and Avenida Santa Fe in the *barrio norte* of Buenos Aires. She recalled being thrilled by Borges's *Ficciones* and surprised when they met through Estela Canto at how different he was in person from the image she had from his prose. Here was a timid, stuttering, blind man, with a featureless, soft face and a waving right hand, while his prose was tough, stripped of ornament, with odd adjectives and verbs; a Spartan concision, she wrote. She was 32 and he 55. They saw each other perhaps once a week for the rest of his life, a friendship without any physical attraction. She was one of the few people who knew him backwards, an 'entrañable amiga' ('bosom friend') said Fanny the maid.[35] He lived with his mother, in his tiny room with ascetic bed and small bookcase (and not one of his own books there). He really lived out-of-this-world; scorned newspapers and the radio; had no idea about footballers (the Argentine passion) and never boasted. When the Queen of Spain sent him a telegram

Alicia Jurado, Borges and the American poet Willis Barnstone. p140, 145

announcing his winning of the Cervantes prize in 1980, he asked
Alicia Jurado, who is this Sofía? Above all, during many walks,
Alicia Jurado revived Borges's absurdist humour, his crazy Lewis
Carroll logic. She had never laughed with anyone more than with
Borges, she said.[36] When he lectured on Buddhism, she recalled,
Perón allocated police spies to report on anything he might say,
who dozed while he spoke because they were so bored.

1

Buenos Aires to Palermo

Not the English one

P 78

Borges was born on 24 August 1899 on calle Tucumán 840 in his maternal grandmother's downtown house in Buenos Aires. It was winter, which in Buenos Aires can be damp and feel far colder than it actually is (though snow has been recorded only twice). This birthplace makes Borges a genuine *porteño*, born in the port that looks outwards to Europe and that swallowed up millions of immigrants who would alter the identity of the country over the late nineteenth century. From the day of his birth, then, Borges inherited a European nostalgia. He has often commented that he felt like a European in exile. His bookish culture was predominantly English and European and his later omnivorous, impatient reading into several European literatures comes from his birthright.

The actual house on calle Tucumán has been demolished. Buenos Aires is a city linked to the pickaxe, for it has turned its past into building rubble to rebuild according to the latest fashions. Borges's birthplace was typically colonial. A single-storey house with a high façade, a tall entrance hall (*zaguán*), inner patios – the first one tiled – with a well, a vine and water tank (*aljibe*) that even had turtles in it to keep the water free from mosquito larvae. On the front door a knocker (for there were no doorbells yet). Borges has often written poems about living in this traditional colonial house, though he moved with his parents to their own house when he was two years old. The building that replaced this house is today a Borges centre, with a blue plaque.

From the day of his birth Borges also inherited what would be the defining physical limitation in his life, first myopia and then a gradual blindness, from his father with the same name, Jorge. Borges himself would have eight eye operations to try and save his sight and was the sixth recorded generation to suffer from blindness. There must be a psychology for all myopes. They see what is close at hand – print, illustrations –and the rest is vague. It would also lead to timidity. Borges was not a descriptive writer because he was a myope. A later epigone and critic, Ricardo Piglia, suggested that Borges's myopia was a kind of magnifying glass that generated Borges's unique way of intense close reading. The threat of blindness was exacerbated by an accident due to his poor eyesight in 1938 that almost led to his death. Only after this accident, to which I shall be returning, did Borges begin to compose the fictions that would make him world-famous (before that he has been a poet and a critic). Fear of incipient blindness preyed on his mind as he knew that memory would become his window on to the world, and few writers have played with memory more acutely than Borges. 'I remember', he wrote, 'is a sacred verb.'[1] For a reader, blindness is a special curse. Borges didn't learn Braille; he memorized reams of poetry and prose by heart, loved being read to and after 1955 composed by dictating. Pre-blindness Borges and post-blindness Borges are different writers because the latter could not see what he had just written, but had to hear it. Borges has written memorably on his blindness, on his links with Homer, Milton and Joyce, and it even affected his strange love-life. He told the American poet and translator Willis Barnstone that the 'blind are forbidden darkness. I live in the centre of a luminous mist.'[2] This doomed unfolding from myopia to final blindness was born with Borges.

Borges was also born a writer. 'I was expected to be a writer', he wrote in his memoirs.[3] There were no self-doubts about becoming a writer; it was his destiny. Not only was his father a frustrated writer, who finally published his sole novel *El caudillo* ('The Boss') in

1920 and translated *The Rubáiyát* of Omar Khayyám for his son's literary journal *Proa* in 1925, but his mother became his best critic and translated D. H. Lawrence, Herbert Read, Faulkner and Kafka. In his family tree were earlier, respectable writers (especially the Lafinurs). Borges's younger sister Norah Borges became a painter, and married one of Spain's most influential literary critics, Guillermo de Torre, who was also an avant-garde poet (an *ultraísta*). A cousin, Guillermo Juan Borges, militated in the local avant-garde. Reading, books, the family library, literary friends, writing and book-talk dominated Borges's life from his infancy. He could not have been anything else but a writer (he was also a librarian and a university teacher, but these later jobs derived from this ontological certainty that he was born a writer).

Borges also inherited an austerity, a scorn for wealth and luxury, especially from the lineage of his mother, Leonor Acevedo Suárez (1876–1975), who came from a family of once-rich landowners (in San Nicolás) who had lost their land. They were *hidalgos pobres*, the shabby genteel, those who mask their poverty with courtesy and culture. He was always simple in his routines, a gent who dismissed the body and its sensual functions as irritants to the life of the mind.

Borges, eldest son, was close to both parents, and much psycho-analytical speculation has come from this dutiful son syndrome. He lived at home, in the same narrow iron bed where he did much of his reading, until his mother died at the age of 99 in 1975, and he Borges was nearly 76 years old and blind. This remaining at home until married was the social norm in Catholic families in Buenos Aires. Everything was done for him so that he could read and write and live that writer's life in cafés and on the streets, be that *flâneur* that he was before he went blind.

His mother has been seen as the terrible, castrating Mother, who insisted on Borges returning home to eat dinner at home and who made it her business to read all that he wrote, and often censured it. In the memoir that Borges wrote in English with Norman

P. 120

Thomas di Giovanni, he is kind about his interfering, snobbish,
Catholic mother, who had once been placed under house arrest ✗
by Perón (Borges's sister Norah actually spent a month in prison).
From his mother Borges inherited a belief that his family was the
backbone of the newly liberated Argentina. In a poem he recalled
these ancestors as soldiers and landowners, descended from
Saxons, Arabs and Goths.[4] Borges's ancestor worship is also political, for all fought the tyrant Rosas as *unitarios*, like his maternal
grandfather Isidoro Acevedo who died in exile in Montevideo in
1905.[5] This praise of ancestors culminated in several dull poems
recounting minor incidents of bravery in battle, poems which
made Borges himself feel urban, inadequate, a coward. One such
was Col. Isidoro Suárez, a maternal great-grandfather who fought
in the battle of Junín of 1824 in Andean Peru and was praised by
the liberator Simón Bolívar. Another was on his father's side, a Col.
Francisco Borges,[6] who apparently let himself be killed, an hon-
ourable suicide, in the battle of La Verde in 1874 (though actually
he was shot by bullets). This patriotic family worship came
through his mother. Estela Canto, the sexy dedicatee of Borges's
marvellous story 'The Aleph', wrote a cruel biography about her
bizarre relationship with Borges. At its core was Borges's refusal
to sleep with her even though she offered herself. It was Borges's
mother Leonor who broke up the relationship by insisting on chap-
eroning Estela every time she went to their home (but in reality
protecting her son). Estela Canto evoked Leonor as tiny, black-
eyed, with the same flabby face as Borges. Without her dedication
to his well-being, she wrote, Borges would not have been a writer.
Borges never questioned his mother's zealous guardianship, didn't
see that it ruined their relationship, never saw her cruelty, her
unbreakable power drive.[7] Atypically, he always called her 'madre',
rather than 'mamá', while he remained 'Georgie'. Alicia Jurado, on
the other hand, thought that Leonor had been slandered by biographers; her devotion to her blind husband and then blind son was

faultless. Leonor dictated her memoirs to Alicia Jurado, who later found them to be too jumbled to be worth typing up. When she died, Borges left her tidy room exactly as it was, with its mahogany bed and family portraits. He would return home and stand in the door and still tell her empty room what he had done. Emir Rodríguez Monegal told a now famous anecdote about being invited to lunch by Borges's mother. Monegal was 25, a literary critic and married. Borges was 47, but unmarried and so still at home. Monegal was offered wine with the meal, but the maid asked his mother if Borges, 'el niño' ('child'), could have any.[8] This maid, Epifanía Uveda de Robledo, found this mother 'very authoritarian'.[9]

Borges was also generous about his father Jorge Guillermo (1874–1938), whom he called a kind man, a philosophical anarchist, at odds with the pretensions of his wife. He was half English thanks to his mother Fanny Haslam, born in Staffordshire, whose father travelled to Argentina to edit the first English newspaper there. Borges inherited a quaint Edwardian English, spoken at home, from his father and grandmother. This father was an easy-going and lazy lawyer and lecturer, who brought his family with him to Europe for an eye operation in 1914 and then had to wait out the First World War abroad. He later went blind and had to stop working. At the end of his life an operation restored his sight. In a poem called 'Buenos Aires', Borges recalled this particular joy: 'It's the pavement of Quintana street where my father, who had been blind, cried because he saw the ancient stars',[10] a miracle that wouldn't happen to Borges. He also inherited his father's passion for metaphysics and psychology (Berkeley, Hume, William James) and reading about the East (Lane, Burton). He also acquired his father's passion for consulting dictionaries and encyclopaedias, a very un-Spanish habit. Strangely for an Argentine, his father was also a vegetarian. Much of Borges's sarcasm and critical scepticism can be seen as a dialogue with his more naïve, idealist and sincere father. Borges's simultaneous admiration for and mocking of idealism is derived from continuous son–father arguments. Borges's constant references to Zeno's paradox came from chess games with his father.[11] Borges also inherited his father's close intellectual friend Macedonio Fernández, who Borges acknowledged as his mentor, a café Socrates who preferred reading and arguing to writing. Borges would be with Macedonio as much as he could, meeting every Saturday evening at La Perla, a café in the Once *barrio*. Borges doesn't mention in his memoirs that his father, a womanizer and unhappily married, also initiated his son sexually, by taking him to a brothel in Geneva and obliging his son to fornicate with his own mistress (the boy wasn't aroused and failed the test). Borges's distaste for sexuality, as reflected in his work, has been marked by this experience, however one interprets the consequences. Borges's mother said that when Borges read poems aloud he sounded exactly like his father. The fundamental paternal inheritance, however, was becoming a writer, for Borges senior's novel *El caudillo* led to his son deriding lengthy novels, even boasting that he had never finished reading one. However, his father was also a poet (publishing sonnets in the magazine *Nosotros*), a translator and destroyed a play titled *Hacia la nada* ('Towards Nothing'). His father's advice to his son was to read a lot, write a lot, destroy a lot and don't rush into print; his father followed his own advice to his son. Much has been made of Borges's parricidal tendencies, his sense of being a nobody, his father's ghost, and more psychoanalytical speculations. However, I see this father as a literary encourager, much as Edmund Gosse's and V. S. Naipaul's fathers were to them.

So when Borges was born in 1899 he inherited becoming a writer, worshipping his ancestors, admiring the English writers and speculating lazily in cafés from his parents. On his mother's side, the local heroes who fashioned independent Argentina still lived on in family lore; on his father's side, foreignness, books, English as the language spoken at home and a dreamy bohemian way of life. Here we have another version of the two Borgeses – the rift between his parents inside him. The fiction 'The South' (first published in the newspaper *La Nación* in 1953), one of Borges's favourite stories, opens with a self-definition that is obviously biographical. Its protagonist is Juan Dahlmann, grandson of Johannes, a German vicar who landed in Buenos Aires in 1871. Juan felt 'hondamente argentino' ('deeply Argentine'), despite the surname. The story develops that deep sense of being an Argentine, tracking that change from Johannes to Juan. His maternal grandfather was Francisco Flores, who died lanced by the famous nomadic Indian leader Catriel. To die for one's country proves one's patriotism and becomes the secret theme of this tale. Dahlmann acknowledges 'discord in his lineage', but chooses his maternal side's Romantic death in action. All that's left of this heroic past is a daguerreotype of Flores, an inexpressive man with a beard, his old sword, the joy of certain songs and the habit of quoting from the 1872 gaucho narrative protest poem *Martín Fierro* that became the nearest thing to a national epic. Borges calls this a 'criollismo algo voluntario' ('somewhat artificial Creole identity'),[12] yet Dahlmann had clung on to family land in the south, with its eucalyptus trees and large faded pink house on the pampas. This story's opening is wonderfully precise about Borges's own dual allegiances, and his own preference for his mother's Argentine heroes over his Germanic (read English) father. For quite a while, as we'll see, Borges exaggerated his 'criollismo', belonging to that creole or colonial Argentina before immigration and cattle wealth altered the country for ever. In 1974 Borges dedicated his complete works to his mother, especially her memories of the patios, the slaves, the charge of the hussars in Peru and Rosas's ignominy, all historical insights about a newly independent Argentina.[13] As we'll see later, his story 'The South' is also about the failure to live up to this heroism. Borges had trouble with such a version of manliness. He felt ashamed, he wrote in his autobiography, of being a bookish man, a coward and not a man of action.

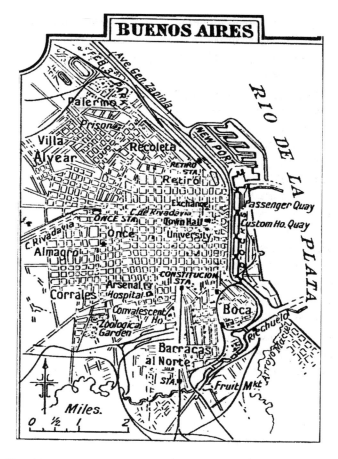

Map of Buenos Aires in 1927.

In 1901, aged two, Borges, with his family, moved to Palermo, a *barrio* (immigrant neighbourhood) at the edge of Buenos Aires, near where the dirty Maldonado stream trickled. At first they lived in calle Serrano 2135, and then built a house in the same street on 2147, both now demolished. The street today has been renamed in his honour and is a trendy area of restaurants, low houses and shady streets. His home was one of the few two-storied houses in Palermo, a poor and modest district, far from the snobby *barrio norte*, for the Borgeses, with a blind and unemployed father, were down on their luck. There were compensations, especially the nearby Botanical Gardens and the Zoo, as we'll see. It's in this house that Borges's personal memories begin. But what is curious in his works is the paucity of references to his infancy and childhood. No Wordsworthian eulogies to the freedom of instincts. Estela Canto noted that Borges was loquacious, but never talked about his infancy.[14] In fact, Borges was confined to his garden with its tall palm tree, its reddish paving-stones, its vine with black grapes, its lance-shaped railings and red windmill (to draw water up from the well), recalled in a poem.[15] He played with his tomboy younger sister Norah, who was born there, and he endlessly read in his father's library. Myopic, shy, stuttering and frail, Borges could not be let out into the rough streets in this *barrio* controlled by thugs and pimps. He was educated at home with an English governess called Miss Tink until he was over eleven years old. In 1970 Borges recalled his time in Palermo, and shrinks it to a library. He wrote: 'If I were asked to name the chief event in my life, I should say my father's library. In fact, I sometimes think I have never strayed outside that library.'[16] Libraries become sacred places of peace and escape throughout his life. So childhood memories become countless books in English and illustrations from encyclopaedias. It's here that the brothers Grimm, Lewis Carroll, Stevenson, Burton and Wells invaded Borges's young mind and lodged there. He also learnt the thrill of illicit reading, for his mother banned *Martín Fierro*, the verse narrative about a lawless gaucho on the run, which he read secretly in the attic, and he also read Burton's unexpurgated translation of *The Arabian Nights*. Around seven years old, Borges began writing by imitating classic writers in Spanish, like Cervantes, with 'La visera fatal' ('The Fatal Helmet') in 1906. It was even argued that he read Cervantes first in English, but he denied it, though to read him later in any edition but Garnier's was to read a different author (a joke he would elaborate in 'Pierre Menard, Author of *Don Quixote*'). He translated Oscar Wilde's 'The Happy Prince' in 1908 and had it published in a Buenos Aires newspaper so that family friends thought that his father had done it. So his first publication was a translation (Borges would develop translation as a key aspect of the literary life). From eleven years old, Borges was sent to school in the nearby Thames street (but not named after London's river) and recalled being bullied because he was dressed by his mother in an Eton collar and tie.

What Borges owed most to Palermo was his lifelong fascination with crime and lower class life. He overheard the gossip of the streets from his island home, and his imagination worked with these snippets. He loved reading the crime novels of the local writer Eduardo Gutiérrez as a boy and in 1930 he would write a quirky biography of the local poet Evaristo Carriego, who lived nearby on calle Honduras 3784 and dropped round to chat with his father. Carriego's house is today a museum and Poetry Centre. Borges thrilled to tango, to gang life in nearby Tierra del Fuego (today a transvestite area). But it was the whole *barrio* that excited Borges; from his enforced respectability, he was spying on real life in the immigrant city. The opening chapter of this avant-garde biography *Evaristo Carriego* is a history of Palermo. The second chapter is about the poet Carriego, born in 1883 and who died young of TB in 1912, with one book *Misas herejes* (1908), published in his lifetime. Borges quickly subverts chronology (in his Buddhist way), saying that it's best to seek out repetitions, eternity. He added: 'Sólo una descripción intemporal, morosa con amor, puede devolvérnoslo' ('Only a timeless description, sluggish with love, can bring it back to us').[17] He outlines Carriego's reading, strangely close to Borges's own, sharing reading *Martín Fierro* clandestinely, and also loving Gutiérrez's stories about *guapos* (thugs). Mostly, Carriego reread Cervantes. But Carriego related to toughs in the area, especially the local boss Nicolás Paredes, evoked by an admiring Borges as the archetypal man, with his long black, insolent hair, his huge moustache and his arrogant stroll. Borges met this man Paredes once. In a poem 'Variación', published in *Sur* in 1970, he thanked this 'old assassin' who lived in a tumbledown room on calle Cabrera and who gave him an orange, saying nobody left his home empty-handed.[18] Carriego himself once dedicated a poem to Borges after telling him about his knife-fighting friends: 'A usté, compañero Borges, Lo saludo enteramente' ('To you, companion Borges, I greet you entirely'), thus initiating Borges into this mythic danger-zone.[19] Carriego would drop by every Sunday with a guitar, and was loathed by Borges's prim mum. This wasn't Borges's only brush with the rough life. In 1934 he was a bystander at a murder in a bar in Rivera, Uruguay, in the border lands with Brazil, with his cousin the writer Enrique Amorim. At least, it happened at a table nearby while he was philosophizing, as he said, and didn't notice.

The opening poem of his third collection of poems, *Cuaderno San Martín* (1929) – the title refers modestly to a school exercise book as well as to the Liberator – is sarcastically titled (to be strict, retitled) 'Fundación mítica de Buenos Aires' ('Mythical Founding of Buenos Aires'). Borges relocates the landing of the city's founder Juan Díaz (de Solís, murdered by Indians in 1516) in his own *barrio* and not where serious historians have guessed, further to the south in La Boca on the muddy Riachuelo river. No, Buenos Aires began and can best be found between the streets of Guatemala, Serrano (where the Borgeses lived), Paraguay and Gurruchaga. Here's Borges's reality: pink-painted stores, men playing *truco*, a gambling card game with its own deck and symbols, hard-faced *compadritos*. You can hear street organs, tangos, Italians (called *gringos* by Borges and most Argentines at that time), and all backed Hipólito Yrigoyen, the Radical political party boss who was ousted by a military coup in 1930.[20] Both the biography of Carriego and the poem

were written by a Borges who discovered nostalgia for Palermo
when he was abroad in Geneva. Borges told fellow writer Ernesto
Sábato that he had set all his stories in the Palermo of the end of
the nineteenth century.[21]

Lastly, his 'essentially indoors' years in Palermo were punctuated
by summer holidays in Uruguay in February, where the Borges's
stayed with Leonor's cousins the wealthy Haedos in their villa near
Montevideo or at their *estancia* ('estate') San Francisco near Fray
Bentos. There Borges learnt about country life, horse skills and
even knife-fights, for he continued to stay with his cousin Esther
Haedo when she married the communist novelist Enrique Amorim
and lived in Salto. There are many references in his works to these
Uruguayan places (Funes, the farm-worker with the perfect memory,
hails from here). During these Uruguayan days Borges swam
in the river. Swimming was the only sport he enjoyed and floating
freed him from his awkward body; it was pure happiness. He wrote
a poem to the fourth element to affirm that 'all men have swum
in the Ganges'; to swim in a river in Geneva or Salto is a sacred
gesture. The poem ends addressing water: 'Remember Borges, your
swimmer, your friend. / Do not fail on my lips in my last moment.'[22]
The family also summered in Adrogué, on the coast south of
Buenos Aires, where they first rented a house and then lodged in a
Hotel Las Delicias, also demolished. In a poem Borges recalled its
garden, its arbours, its jasmines, reading Verlaine, and especially
the medicinal smell of the eucalyptus, ubiquitous Argentine trees
imported from Australia. He evokes the hotel itself, with mica
sheets of grey stone, mirrors, a lion's head biting a large ring and
windows stained with red and green glass. This exact hotel resur-
faced in the 1942 detective story 'Death and the Compass'. By then,
Borges had begun his pastiche detective stories with his friend
Adolfo Bioy Casares, in which their invented cop don Isidro Parodi
wallowed in the atmosphere Borges absorbed from the Palermo of
his adolescence.

One memory from Palermo followed Borges through his life, that of watching the Bengal tiger in the Zoo. The Zoo, with its main entrance on Plaza Italia from where calle Serrano starts, was opened in 1888 and was wildly exotic, with Hindu temples and lakes, and a fake Vesta temple. Family lore has Borges refusing to come home, transfixed by the caged beast behind bars. His tiny mother was scared of her burly son's tantrums, and could hardly pull him home. Her punishment for these moments of rebellion was to ban his books. This real tiger developed into one of Borges's keenest insights about the interplay between the mind and empirical reality. He wrote a prose piece with an English title 'Dreamtigers' in 1934 under the pseudonym Francisco Bustos (republished in 1960), where he claimed: 'I was a fervent worshipper of the tiger.'[23] This is not the local jaguar or puma from the floating islands of the Paraná, but the stripped, Asiatic royal creature. Comparing what he imagined from reading about tigers in Kipling's *The Jungle Book* or seeing them illustrated in encyclopaedias with what he saw with his five senses, Borges was able to oppose the tiger on the page with the tiger in the cage. He realized, sadly, how they blurred and how we are left always with images of something that was once more real. From these 'dream tigers' he could never create a real one; they ended up as dogs or birds. In a later poem titled 'The panther', Borges surmises that the trapped panther cannot guess that there are deer in the mountains awaiting his blind appetite. We are all caged in ourselves.[24] Rilke's panther from the Paris zoo is equally trapped behind its thousand bars, its mighty will paralysed, but life still darts inwards into its heart. The living tiger is a mirror of our living animal self, a feline Don Juan, a 'macho', in the poet Rubén Darío's words.[25]

In the same 1960 collection, *El hacedor*, Borges published 'El otro tigre' ('The other tiger'), which opens with 'I think of a tiger', a mental tiger which lives in a world without names or past or future, just 'un instante cierto' ('an instant of certainty').[26] But he confesses that this inner tiger is symbolic, a shadow, a literary trope, while the hot-blooded Sumatran one continues its routines of love, death and idleness. The poet's impotence in creating a tiger haunts him, for it lies outside the poem. By then, too, he was blind. The poem 'El oro de los tigres' ('The gold of the tigers') again refers back to the Bengal cat in the Zoo in Palermo and William Blake's 'Tyger tyger burning bright'. The poet's anxious hands yearn to stroke its precious golden hair. For the beast's vibrant body reminded sightless Borges of all that once throbbed and that only his blind man's hands could touch.

In 1950 Borges added a prologue to his 1930 biography of Carriego (further evidence of Borges's lack of respect for chronology), and argued, brilliantly, that Carriego created the image that *porteños* now have of their *barrios*, so that his writings modified their perceptions of reality. Borges lived in Carriego's same 'mediocre arrabal sudamericano' ('mediocre South American neighbourhood'), but learnt a crucial truth from his forgotten local poet.[27] This Carriego read Dumas, convinced that real life lay abroad in France. Borges realized that the centre of the universe is experienced at any moment in any place, there in the mere present of Palermo, 1904. That is, subjectively, the only universe you can know is the centre of the universe. In the *arrabal* ('city slum') of Palermo Borges discovered, citing Heraclitus of Ephesus, 'Enter, for here too are the Gods.' No such thing as being in the periphery. Suddenly his lowly, ignored Palermo has its gods, its myths, its sacred centre. It was here too that Borges first experienced 'eternity'. In a deleted piece of 1926 titled 'Dos esquinas' ('Two street corners'), Borges set off for one of his aimless walks through back streets, what's called *caminar al azar* (a Surrealist practice), and found himself by the Maldonado stream (that is, in Palermo), a place that he had possessed in words but not in reality; he was in the wrong side of familiar Buenos Aires with low, poor houses, pink walls, fig trees and mud, American mud, he wrote, and a state of bizarre, utter happiness. Nothing had changed in twenty years: a bird sings, a cricket scratches, silence is vertiginous. 'Me sentí muerto' ('I felt dead'), he wrote, outside time, in one of those impersonal states like pleasure, or falling asleep, with successive time a delusion. This crucial experience lies at the source of his work and being.

Borges recreated his shattering insight about the centre being where you happen to be in a short prose piece called 'La trama' ('The Plot'), where Julius Caesar cries out '¡Tú también, hijo mío!' ('You too, my son!') as Brutus stabs him, repeated in Buenos Aires province by a gaucho who says ('you must say it aloud', writes Borges), 'Pero, che!' (that 'che' metonymically Argentine). He dies so that Caesar's scene in Shakespeare ('Et tu, Brute') and Quevedo is repeated.[28] Here, a typical Borges insight: Quevedo is Shakespeare's equal, but nobody acknowledges this; he wrote an essay 'Quevedo' (1948) trying to explain this ignorance and refers to Quevedo's 1631 commentary on Plutarch's *Marco Bruto*. The archetype of betrayal is just as real in Argentina as it is anywhere else in the world. There is no centre but where you stand, now. Borges does the same in 'Story of the Warrior and the Captive Maiden' where his English grandmother (Fanny Haslam) meets a Yorkshire woman kidnapped by the nomadic Indians, but who stayed on with them. She would leap off a horse to drink a mare's hot blood. She completely renounced her English birthright, just like Drotfulft who changed sides and fought for the Romans in Ravenna. Borges's grandmother at a military frontier post and the English woman illustrated the same secret impulse. In Argentina and in Italy, they're one side of the same coin from God's point of view (again Borges leaps into eternity).

The *barrio* of Palermo returned in a late story called 'Juan Muraña' from *El informe de Brodie* (*Brodie's Report*) of 1970, dictated when blind. Borges, his own character, summarizes his Palermo origins, the garden, the library, the Carriego biography. In a train on the way to Morón, Borges meets an old school friend from calle

Thames days called Trápani who had taught the prim Borges 'lunfardo', Buenos Aires underworld slang. This same Trápani said that he had read Borges's Carriego biography, harping on about thugs. 'Decime, Borges, vos, ¿qué podés saber de malevos?' ('Tell me, Borges, what on earth do you know about thugs?'). Borges defends himself: I based it all on documents. There is a silence and the old school mate announces, 'I was Juan Muraña's nephew.' Muraña existed, was a folk hero. He tells a story about his widowed aunt who quietly slips out of their house in the pasaje Russell (it exists) and stabs the landlord about to evict them. She had enigmatically said that Juan, her late husband, would not let a *gringo* leave them roofless. But he had been dead ten years. Instead she had taken his dagger, symbol of the man and his guts. It was the dagger which killed the *gringo* not the old widow. This aunt's husband, her 'tiger', is now the memory of a knife, and soon will vanish into oblivion.[29] That is, Muraña was a forgettable thug, only important to a young Borges trapped inside respectability. Palermo, in the 71-year-old Borges, still reverberated with crime. Did this encounter really happen to Borges or was bumping into Trápani a literary device?

2

Geneva and Spain

In 1914, naïvely unaware of impending war, the Borgeses, with the maternal grandmother, decided to rent their Palermo house and sail by German steamer to Europe for an operation on Borges's father's failing eyesight. Living in Europe would be cheaper, too. They reached Geneva at the end of April 1914 and stayed in 17 Rue Malagnou until 6 June 1918 when war ended and they left for Lugano and then Mallorca. These four war years trapped in neutral Switzerland were crucial to Borges's intellectual independence. It was there that he read Schopenhauer and Verlaine's 'magical music' in the original, for he picked up French, German and Latin, reading at ease in five languages (he already had Spanish and English). He had become a polyglot. He was happy there, studied at the Collège Calvin, in the French system, but never completed his Swiss baccalauréat.[1] He also discovered avant-garde art and German Expressionist poetry, distilled by him into a poetics of vehemence, abundance of imagery and a belief in universal brotherhood, but he disparaged Tzara's Dada in nearby Zurich as public exhibitionism. His intellectual development and confidence grew astoundingly, and can be followed in his letters to his Jewish Genevan school friend Maurice Abramowicz.

Borges told César Fernández Moreno in 1969 that Geneva was like home, a city that he knew better than Buenos Aires because of its natural size, and because he was young there (and later capriciously chose to die there). However, reading and literary friendships

Jorge Guillermo Borges, his wife Leonor Acevedo Suárez, and their children, Jorge Luis and Norah, on the eve of their departure to Geneva in 1914.

were beginning to define his life. He discovered Walt Whitman in a German translation, immediately ordered the *Leaves of Grass* and boasted that he had 'met' Whitman in Geneva. He became a Whitmaniac (Borges approved of Swinburne's nickname). Whitman became the 'only' poet, so that Borges's first published poem 'Hymn to the Sea' in a Spanish avant-garde magazine called *Grecia* in December 1919 (Borges was 21) was described by him as 'I tried my hardest to be Walt Whitman'.[2] His future brother-in-law Guillermo de Torre said that when he first met him, Borges was 'drunk on Whitman'. That Whitman was American in a Europe dominated by the Parisian avant-garde was a clue to Borges's fascination (the American Revolution antedated the French, he wrote). He wrote in an essay 'The other Whitman' in which he appreciated Whitman's sense that intellectual schemes are invalid in contrast with the 'primary news from the senses'. Whitman's message to Borges: 'Unexpected and elusive is the world, but its very contingency is a richness, as we cannot even determine how poor we are, given that everything is a gift.'[3] In Geneva, Borges was an anti-intellectual vitalist.

In another essay on Whitman, Borges touched on happiness, and again on the nature of biography, that split between Whitman the 'vagabundo feliz' ('happy vagabond') of the poems and Whitman the 'pobre literato' ('poor literary hack') who wrote them.[4] Borges would develop that notion of 'vagabond' on his return to Buenos Aires. Whitman wanted to be all men, and found a way of chatting with his future readers, a friend, happiness itself. Borges defined Whitman's genius as having created a triple hero: the biographical Whitman; his self-creation in the poem, also called Whitman; and the reader's invention of his or her own 'Whitman'. There's not a page when this triple Whitman is not present. As Borges conversed with this hero, 'a momentary identification' turned Borges into Whitman.[5] Here is the source of a Borges's reader's psychology, the two or three Borgeses, and his escape from biography. So, Borges in Geneva and through Whitman discovered the freedom of the senses and a way of writing that presumed both a loss of individuality and an acquiring of democracy where we are all equal. In a later sonnet, 'Camden 1892', the poet Borges speaks through Whitman, 'Casi no soy, pero mis versos ritman / La vida y su esplendor' ('I hardly am, but my poems rhyme with life and its splendours') to end 'I was Whitman'.[6] In 1969, still faithful to his Genevan discovery, Borges translated and prologued an anthology of *Hojas de hierba* (*Leaves of Grass*). To attain happiness through reading and writing became a drive. He quoted the Argentine-born naturalist W. H. Hudson who many times in his life began to study metaphysics, but was always interrupted by a bout of happiness. Borges called this one of the 'most beautiful sentences' in the world,[7] only I could never locate it in Hudson's works. Did he invent this Hudson quotation?

Geneva was also, as I've hinted, where Borges was initiated into sex with a whore in a brothel by his father (and nothing happened). As Estela Canto confirms, this brothel act was to probe Borges's manliness. Years later, she was invited by Borges's psychotherapist Dr Cohen-Miller (in reality, Kohan-Miller) to come to a session with Borges himself, who was not impotent but was panicked by the idea of sex with a woman, and felt shame.[8] This revelation was shocking in 1986, but Canto went further: she had offered herself to him as a lover, but he, ever the gent, only wanted marriage. Yet she felt his 'excitement' through his trousers.[9] How traumatic

cf 125·26

that Genevan incident was can only be guessed at, but I can read Borges's experience into one of his few female characters, Emma Zunz. Borges had chosen the name for its ugliness (he also disliked Flaubert's Emma Bovary). In this strange story of reversing chronology, Emma seeks to avenge her father's exile by killing a Jewish factory owner. In order to claim that he had raped her, she went down to the infamous Paseo de Julio, picked up a Finnish or Swedish sailor, let him copulate with her, and then went off to kill her father's tormentor. About copulation we read: 'She thought (she couldn't not help thinking) that her father had done to her mother the horrible thing being done now to her. She thought it with a weak-limbed astonishment, and then, immediately took refuge in vertigo.'[10] Sex, then, is the vile thing that her father did to her mother. She had to think because she was being raped like her mother, then she became giddy (with pleasure?). The war between men and women at that time is relived by Emma (what a mockery of Jane Austen) and Borges too as he wrote this extraordinary insight into the primal scene. This story was turned into a film by Torre Nilson in 1954, *Días de odio*. In his 1952 story 'The Cult of the Phoenix' the sect of the title is so widespread that its 'secret' has been forgotten. It's more a punishment practised to prolong generations and can be taught by anybody, even a boy. This forgotten secret is obviously linked with D. H. Lawrence; the phoenix as the penis. In fact, this trivial, momentary and sacred act, associated with mud and renounced by mystics, could be masturbation. Few have caught on to the joke. Borges told Ronald Christ that the secret was copulation, and that he'd been shocked at the thought of his parents doing it (like Emma Zunz).[11]

Estela Canto did not doubt that Borges slept with some women; Borges boasted in a letter of 1921 that after winning at roulette, he spent three nights in a brothel with a woman nicknamed La Princesa.[12] But this has not silenced critics about the nature of his unconfessed sexual life. My guess is that the infrequency of references to women or sex in his stories is due more to reserve than absence of libido. My own key lies in the final poem of his third collection *Cuaderno San Martín* (1929), which is titled 'Paseo de Julio' (an actual street today renamed Avenida Leandro Alem) that links back to his story 'Emma Zunz'. This street of whores and tango music is so vile that it cannot be part of his 'patria'. All happiness, wrote the poet, is hostile to this street, which in the original ending of the poem is heaven for those who live in hell (Buenos Aires's brothels). By 1929 Borges had separated love from sex. This is the core of his Romantic longing for love, contaminated by actual sexuality. In October 1921 Borges wrote a daring prose piece on the front page of the Spanish avant-garde magazine *Ultra* called 'Casa Elena' (an actual brothel in Mallorca), subtitled 'Towards an aesthetics of brothels in Spain' (he used the word 'lupanar' for brothel, from the root meaning wolf).[13] Aged 23, he offers us a theory of love. In brothels all religions fail and Adam and Eve are reduced to merchandise and buyers. Pleasure has failed, has been mutilated, robbed of its 'romantic vision'.[14] Love can be bought with rusty fake coins. However, this is brothel sex. In this same piece, Borges defends the carnal tryst, and its orgasmic intensity that can never be caught by art. For 'pleasure is all that matters and nobody will ever trap it in the plot of art'. He knew about sexual pleasure, but couldn't match it with his Romantic version of love. There are a few surprising moments in his work alluding to the bliss and pain of sexuality. In 1960 he hid behind Gaspar Camerarius, a fake Latin poet, and wrote 'Le regret d'Heraclite': 'Yo, que tantos hombres he sido, no he sido nunca / aquel en cuyo abrazo desfallecía Matilde Urbach' ('I who so many men have been, have never been that one in whose embrace Matilde Urbach fainted'), possibly regretting that he didn't sleep with Estela Canto.[15] The title reflects his fascination with the pre-Socratic philosopher Heraclitus's fragment: Nobody goes down twice to the waters of the same river; there's no second time; 'my favourite quotation' he said in 1977. In his longest story 'The Congress' (the title is a pun on copulation), the narrator recalls sexual bliss with Beatriz Frost in London, his lover, as a mystical experience: 'From her lips came the word I dared not speak', but doesn't tell us what that word was. It ends with an elegy to warm, shared darkness, flowing love, loss of self and dawn with 'myself contemplating her'.[16] However, contemplation is not possession. The untypical poem 'El amenazado' ('The Threatened Man') of 1972 ends: 'El nombre de una mujer me delata. / Me duele una mujer en todo el cuerpo' ('The name of a woman betrays me / A woman hurts me in all my body').[17] He later excised this aching, physical poem as too personal. Who was this woman?

In his piece called 'Geneva' in *Atlas* (1984), Borges associated Geneva with love, humiliation and the temptation of suicide. Could this refer to his brothel failure? Perhaps not, but earlier in the 1920s Borges did resent his Genevan years. In a self-portrait that he wrote for an 'Exposición de la poesía argentina' ('Exhibition of Argentine Poetry') published in the literary magazine *Martín Fierro* in 1926, he wrote that he spent the war years in Geneva, a period without escape, caged in, that 'I recall always with some loathing'. But, as ever, he refrained from attaching his emotion to incidents. Years later, he would say that he discovered his nostalgia for Buenos Aires in Geneva, where he died and is buried.

After spending a year in Lugano at the Hotel du Lac, and suffering post-war shortages, the Borges family travelled together south to France in 1919, then Mallorca and finally Seville in Andalucia, where they stayed some two and a half months. Jorge Luis was now twenty years old and his sister Norah eighteen. They moved for a while to Madrid in 1920, from March to May, and then ten months in Palma and Valldemosa, Mallorca (where Borges, *père*, self-published his sole novel). In March 1921 they finally sailed back to Buenos Aires on the *Reina Victoria Eugenia*. These Spanish days were one long holiday. Borges's freedom from having to work, his day-long leisure, were granted because 'it was now understood that I should devote myself to writing'.[18] They were also Borges's initiation into the literary life as he befriended the young Spaniards battling for a new art, the tepid, aesthetic Spanish version of Futurism and

Borges and sister Norah with a doctor friend and family on Mallorca, *c.* 1920.

Norah Borges's cover for the magazine *ULTRA*.

Cubism called *Ultraísmo*. Borges was not a leader, did not pen manifestos like the extrovert Chilean Vicente Huidobro who spread avant-garde ideas in Spain in 1918 after living in Paris and befriending Reverdy and Juan Gris, but he had a vitality and freshness that

Jorge Luis Borges. Novedad, en todo, y en todo, verso o prosa, ingenio, talento, solidez mental.

surprise any reader who limits him to his famous stories in the 1940s. At this sunny moment of his life, Borges was a Whitmanish poet and a provocative literary critic.

In Mallorca in 1920 he met and later corresponded with Jacobo Sureda. Through these letters we follow Borges's negotiating his way through the conflicting versions of the avant-garde. He was aware of the Russian Revolution, but remained anti-Bolshevic. He dismissed Vicente Huidobro's pastiches of Apollinaire as being too imitated in Spain and belittled his boasting prose; he rejected the Dadaists as being too deliberately scandalous. He admired Rimbaud (whom he could quote by heart) and defined himself as anti-Mallarmé, or the style of writing where words do not correspond with lived reality. He translated German Expressionist poets.

¶

Out of this omnivorous awareness, Borges started thinking of
how he could combine the avant-garde pressure to be original
and shocking with his love for writing. In a letter to Jacobo Sureda,
Borges decided that his 'ideal book would be metaphysics, *ultraísmo*,
greguerías and a refutation of the book and of its egoisms'.[19] This
avant-garde or Ultraist breaking of genre fitted wonderfully with
Borges's passions: to condense thinking, to reduce poetry to
metaphors, and then to undermine the whole project by refuting it.
The seed to his later *Ficciones* lies in these avant-garde activities.
The untranslatable term 'greguería' is a direct allusion to Ramón
Gómez de la Serna's new genre of wildly humorous one-liners.

In Madrid, Borges and his sister Norah sat on the red divans of
the Café Pombo on Carretas street where the pipe-smoking, sturdy
Ramón Gómez de la Serna directed his *tertulias* every Saturday
night. He had translated Marinetti's Futurist manifesto into Spanish
in 1909, and monopolized, from his corner café table, the arguments
and discussions about the new art (he made all visitors sign a book).
A stuttering Borges would not have got a word in edgeways, but
dynamic Ramón's *greguerías* mixed wit, humour and shock, reduc-
ing the long tradition of Spanish literature to surprising extended
metaphors. Later, he would become a close friend to Macedonio
Fernández, and then Oliverio Girondo, visiting Buenos Aires for
the first time in 1931, and making a beeline for Macedonio's *pensión*.
He then married an Argentine, Luisa Sofovich, and lived in Buenos
Aires, where he also died. Borges was not a close friend to this
garrulous, extrovert, busy man, mass-producing his biographies,
critical notes and one-liners. Borges, in a review, underlined his
'thick, carnal, smothering' vision of life. Back in Buenos Aires,
Borges wrote a piece in the avant-garde magazine *Martín Fierro* in
January 1925 called 'Ramón and Pombo'. He linked Gómez de la
Serna with 'the Alef, which in the new mathematics is the sign for
the infinite figure that includes all the rest'. According to Borges,
Ramón was a Renaissance man who has labelled the world, and not

a 'yawn' in anything that he writes.[20] Ramón (the Aleph, labelling the world) becomes one of the real-life candidates for the fictional poet Daneri so cruelly teased by Borges in his crucial fiction 'The Aleph' (1943). In this story, Carlos Argentino Daneri owns the mystical Aleph under the stairs in a house in humble Garay Street, Buenos Aires, which allows him, and then Borges, to see everything at once. This bad poet wants to capture 'modern man',[21] with his telephones, cinemas and phonographs, and writes a poem titled 'The Earth', enumerating the whole world, starting with some hectares in Queensland, Australia. Borges's wicked mockery of Gómez de la Serna as 'Alef' is hidden (few literary critics have noted this), but in the story this bad poet wins two prizes, the first literary and the second carnal – he beds his cousin Beatriz (originally, Borges had written not 'cousin' but 'sister'). 'The Aleph' is a study in literary and sexual envy. However, Bartolomé Galíndez, a local Argentine poet mocked by Borges as a man of maps, addicted to geographical adventures, applauded by the Futurist Marinetti, a 'monicongo afrancesado de la infraliteratura' ('Frenchified cartoon film of sub-literature'), also lives on in disguise as Carlos Argentino Daneri in 'The Aleph'.[22] An amalgam of both Galíndez and Ramón lurk there. Critics have found other real-life models, including his brother-in-law Guillermo de Torre and even Pablo Neruda, whose *Residencia en la tierra* (1935) covers the world in its title (Neruda and Daneri differ only by a 'u'). Borges and Neruda met while the latter had briefly been consul for Chile in Buenos Aires in 1933 and Neruda had mocked Borges's bookishness. Borges himself said in 1970 that the pompous but fictitious Carlos Argentino Daneri was based on a friend who never guessed he was the target. Nor have the critics, or common readers. However, Borges did not feel close to Ramón, who died a Francoist. Ramón, for his part, saw Borges as 'sly', always contradicting everybody. A very pale Borges to him seemed to spy on life from behind curtains. He was, wrote Gómez de la Serna, 'huraño' ('unsociable'), remote and 'indócil' ('head-

46

strong').[23] Nevertheless, Ramón's review of Borges's first book of
poems in Ortega y Gasset's prestigious *Revista de Occidente* in 1925
started the ball of Borges's European fame rolling.

In Seville, over the winter of 1919/20, Borges published his
Whitman-inspired 'Hymn to the Sea' in *Grecia*, the magazine that
congregated the avant-gardists of that city. Later, in Madrid, Borges
met one of the three living geniuses of his life, the Sevillen Rafael
Cansinos-Asséns (only Borges added the accent) who chose to
become a Jew. Borges often called him 'my master' in that venerable master/disciple tradition. Here was a vastly well-read man,
who knew sixteen languages, had a meditative mind and became
Borges's mentor. He was also the translator of the *Arabian Nights*,
De Quincey, Barbusse and Goethe into Spanish. Years later, Borges
pinpointed his appeal: 'The most remarkable fact about Cansinos
was that he lived completely for literature, without regard for
money or fame.'[24] This literary intensity and dedication, all or
nothing, was adopted by Borges himself. Cansinos-Asséns ran his
tertulias from the café Colonial, where a group of some twenty
young rebels (he'd called them 'disciples') would discuss jazz,
Parisian fads, free verse, the metaphor, despising, Borges wrote,
all that was typically Spanish from flamenco to bull-fighting. They
never discussed contemporary writers. They would meet every
Saturday and argue from midnight to dawn. But most striking was
his library: 'his whole house was a library. It was like making your
way through a wood. He was too poor to have shelves, and the
books were piled one on top of the other from floor to ceiling . . .'[25]
Cansinos's lesson was his un-Spanish Spanish style (he had taught
himself Hebrew) and his 'far-flung' reading. Both terms could be
applied to Borges, whose concise Spanish reads like the English he
spoke bilingually, and who read in bafflingly eclectic ways. Lastly,
Borges learnt how to break out of the solitude of reading and writing: 'What I got from him, chiefly, was the pleasure of literary
conversation.'[26] Borges's extreme love for book-talk was picked up

from these lively café *tertulias*. In 1925, back in Buenos Aires, Borges summarized the avant-garde battles in Madrid between Gómez de la Serna and Cansinos Assens. Both met in their respective cafés and talked until dawn. You had to choose which one to attend. Borges chose the losing side (Assens), for the *greguerías* (Gómez de la Serna) won out. Borges also learnt that Argentines should no longer look to Europe anymore, but must write poems with a 'sabor a patria' ('taste of your country').[27] Later, in a poem dedicated to Cansinos-Assens, he confessed that 'his memory always accompanies me'.[28]

In 1920 in Madrid, Borges also met Guillermo de Torre (1900–1971), his future brother-in-law. According to a close friend and biographer, Borges was unhappy with his marriage to Norah in 1928.[29] De Torre, another leader of the Spanish avant-garde,

Guillermo de Torre and his wife Norah Borges in 1928.

Norah Borges   7 Suárez 7 and whoever

A line drawing of Borges by his sister Norah.

would write the best summary of Spanish attitudes to the competing avant-gardes on offer in 1925 (*Literaturas europeas de vanguardia*). He had taken sides against the Chilean polemicist Huidobro (Borges shared this dislike), accusing him of plagiarizing Pierre Reverdy. When De Torre boasted in *La Gaceta Literaria* in May 1928 that Madrid was the natural cultural centre for the Spanish-speaking world, Borges, with others in the magazine *Martín Fierro*, reacted with anti-Spanish jibes: 'Not in Montevideo, nor in Buenos Aires, as far as I know, is there any sympathy for Spain.' Borges and his friend Carlos Mastronardi also penned a humorous pastiche in the magazine *Martín Fierro*, using thick *lunfardo* slang, and signing themselves Ortelli y Gasset, mocking the famous Madrid philosopher Ortega y Gasset (and associating themselves with Italian immigrants). This was one of the first of many collaborative texts that Borges would write (to break out of the solitude of writing). He nursed a grudge against his brother-in-law all his life. In the family, de Torre was known as being opinionated, 'muy protestón' ('complaining all the time'), self-centred.

Was Borges's resentment concerning his brother-in-law due to losing his sister Norah (1901–1998) in marriage in 1928? Was it that she would start a family, have two sons, when he, Borges, couldn't (inhibited by inherited glaucoma)? Borges wrote little about his relationship with his sister Norah, who illustrated his early poetry books, was a successful artist in her own right, and his sole childhood companion. She was nineteen months younger (born on 4 March 1901) and they were brought up together in the closed world of their Palermo home and given much freedom by their father, who thought that parents should learn from children.[30] In their games and climbing trees, Norah was the tomboy, nicknamed 'El caudillo' ('the Chief'), while he was timid and easily scared. More than anything, Borges shared a complicity of mute glances with his sister, such was their understanding. She hated arguing, did not collect books (indeed, sacrilegiously burnt them when emptying her mother's flat in 1975). Borges persuaded her to write about art in a magazine he edited called *Los Anales de Buenos Aires*, but she only did so under the pseudonym of Manuel Pinedo (as she was also too shy). Borges summed up their deep relationship in 1974: 'we shared silence', he wrote. A critic claimed that his sister Norah was his 'permanent muse', but few biographers have delved into their complicity.[31]

Borges wrote two books in Spain that he destroyed. One was a collection of essays called *Los naipes del tahur* ('Gambler's Cards') under the tough-guy influence of Pío Baroja (this title reappears self-mockingly in his story 'The Aleph'). The second was a book of poems *The Red Psalms* or *The Red Rhythms* (Borges cannot remember exactly). Some of these poems were published in magazines, and praise the Russian Revolution, the brotherhood of man and Borges's bookish anarchistic pacifism, inherited from his father. Borges, the critical reader of his own stuff, was not satisfied. He wrote in a letter to his friend Macedonio Fernández that these psalms were writing themselves.[32] Borges would recall his Spanish years, on his slow way home, as one of receiving 'that splendid Spanish hospitality', and at last speaking Spanish after four years of French in Geneva.[33] He never wrote in French or, bar some later poems, in English.

Borges revived his earlier Genevan self in a late story, 'The Other', that opens *El libro de arena* ('The Book of Sand') of 1970. He, the blind narrator, sits on a bench opposite the Charles River in Boston, where he is lecturing. Somebody sits by him and starts to whistle a tune by Elías Regules (1860–1929, a Uruguayan *milonga* composer). According to María Esther Vázquez, Borges was completely deaf to all music,[34] but this whistling jerks him back to a long-dead cousin, Alvaro Melián Lafinor (1889–1958), who appears as himself in 'The Aleph' and who voted against Borges winning the 1942 prize; Borges doesn't forget his enemies. In this way Borges engages his earlier self, sitting on a similar bench by the Rhone in Geneva. This earlier self still lives at 17 Malagnou, by the Russian church, and lists objects like a silver mate (a gourd to drink yerba maté in) with serpent's claws from Peru, and books, from Lane's *Arabian Nights* to Quicherst's Latin dictionary, to the Garnier edition of *Don Quixote* and a secret book on the sexual habits of the Balkan people. The older Borges reveals that 'mother' still lives, and that 'father' died. He outlines world history since his

Genevan days, and points out that Buenos Aires has become more and more 'provincial'. The earlier self is still writing poems for a book to be called *Los himnos rojos* ('Red Hymns') on brotherly love, but the narrator senses no link between the older and earlier selves: 'we couldn't understand each other'; they are caricatures of each other.[35] The young one doesn't know that blindness is seeing yellow, shadows and lights and nothing else (the older Borges cannot see his earlier self). Time passing is a severing of selves, each one trapped in a past monad, no sense of continuity except for a love of books and 'always bookish references'. The story of two selves is best seen, he writes, as the younger one dreaming and forgetting his dream, while he the ageing Borges was 'tormented by memories'. It's a simply told story, but the reader is not given access to the memories that 'tormented' the aged, blind Borges. The clue must be that they do not talk about 'love'.

Here he should have
brought back Borges, the all-men
of the introduction to characterize
him better & remind the reader.
His characterization here is sketchy.

3

Buenos Aires, the Avant-garde and Literary Friendships

After seven crucial, formative years abroad in Europe Borges, at 22 years old, returned home in March 1921 to Buenos Aires, from what he called his *destierro* ('exile'). Because their Palermo home was rented, the family lived nearby on calle Bulnes 2216 from 1921 to 1923. Borges arrived as a foreigner to his city, bringing the novelties of the latest European literary fashions. In an autobiographical note in 1926 Borges conceived of this return as a 'great mental adventure', rediscovering his city like a prodigal son. In a prologue to the book that captured this intense patriotic joy, *Fervor de Buenos Aires* (1923), Borges defined his poems as praising an actual *porteño* vision of surprising and marvellous places seen during his long walks. For Borges returned a *flâneur*. He strolled everywhere, a walking-thinking that re-enacted the Europeans' first discovery of the New World. In his memoirs Borges noted how determining living abroad had been: 'I wonder whether I would have seen it with the peculiar shock and glow that it now gave me'.[1] However, Borges did not recover a tourist's city; his perspective was peculiar.

The poems he collected in *Fervor de Buenos Aires* suggest a pilgrimage, a quest for belonging, for roots, a fervour that bordered on faith. Borges created his own mental city, best defined as outskirts (*arrabales*), doorways (*zaguanes*), vines, one-storey houses with patios, quiet and empty back streets. In fact, he sought a city that had nothing to do with the European cities he had known. Like Walt Whitman, he sauntered a city free of literary

Norah Borges's woodcuts for Borges's two books of poems: *left* for the cover of *Fervor de Buenos Aires* (1923); *centre and right* for the cover and colophon of *Luna de enfrente* (1925).

and historical associations; he was an Adam naming new things. Borges consciously avoided the new Haussmann-inspired avenues of the centre, the new gory, baroque towers like the Palacio Barolo, and the ornate Jockey Club of the landed class, on calle Florida, built in 1897 and which W. A. Hirst found 'unsurpassed by any club building in the world'. Borges dismissed the Buenos Aires that copied Paris or Madrid. He avoided the modern city and picked a *criollo* or colonial city, before massive immigration and modernity and urban angst defined city-life. So he nosed about Constitución station, the Paternal railway sidings, humble Palermo where he grew up and the Parque Lezama in the slums of *barrio sur*. Borges intuited that real Buenos Aires did not imitate Europe, that its 'involuntarias bellezas' ('unintentional beauties') lay in the outskirts.

And these suburbs had to be won by slowly pacing their empty back streets. In a newspaper article 'Profesión de fe literaria' ('Declaration of Literary Faith') of 1926 he offers a theory of language that issues from experiencing reality: 'I think that words have to be conquered by living them, and the apparent publicity that the dictionary offers is false. Let nobody dare write *suburb* without having walked for a long time along its high pavements . . .'.[2] You have to live first what you later write.

Everybody who knew Borges over the 1920s and 1930s, while his eyesight allowed him to walk unaided, has commented on his long strolls talking books with friends and lovers. Clearly, for Borges the street was freedom; to be on the streets was to escape his mother's vigilance and practice the 'lust of the eyes', that promiscuous brushing with women, those accidents or happenings that also excited the Parisian Surrealists. The opening poem of *Fervor de Buenos Aires* was titled 'Las calles' ('Streets') and the opening lines 'Las calles de Buenos Aires / ya son mi entraña' ('The streets of Buenos Aires / are already my guts').[3] In this first poem, the poet rejects the 'avid' streets in the commercial centre packed with crowds. Borges wrote a forward to this first book that he excised in all later editions, 'A quien leyere' ('To whom may read'), and stated categorically: 'On purpose then, I have rejected the vehement claims of those in Buenos Aires who only notice what is foreign; the noisy energy of the central streets, the universal mobs in the docks.'[4] According to Borges, nobody before had noticed that beauty lay in the empty streets; it's there that Borges 'recovered his inheritance'. He felt this quiet city in his bones. 'The years I have lived in Europe are illusory', he wrote, 'in my dreams I was and will always be in Buenos Aires'.[5] Years later, he repeated that in his dreams he was always in Buenos Aires. In his second and slight book of poems of 1925, *Luna de enfrente* ('Moon across the Street') (it had 42 pages, with a print run of 300), Borges continued with this walking and hallowing of certain corners of the city, his *patria*. He became 'rich in streets', and streets became 'the only music of my life'. The collection's title, made the moon, emblem of poetry, according to Borges's abolished prologue, more urban, more local and familiar.

It was in these city streets that Borges courted, scribbled poems (he never learnt to type) and even plastered posters of an avant-garde magazine on walls. In 1921, bursting with avant-garde passions absorbed in Spain, he co-founded *Prisma*, a mural magazine.

It ran for two numbers (December 1921 and March 1922), and promoted manifestos about *ultraísta* poetics, poems and woodcuts made by Norah, his sister. At night, he scuttled out with his friends and pasted these posters along the main avenues like Santa Fe and Callao. It was almost a family affair, with Norah and cousin Francisco Piñero, while his mother supplied the glue. One of Norah's woodcuts also became the cover for his first book of poems: a low suburban house, with balustrades, hidden patios and nobody about, a Platonic or Chirico-esque Buenos Aires, Borges told Juan Cruz, meaning its perfect archetype, its hidden beauty.[6] Borges had destroyed his *ultraísta* poems; a modern poem should not be dependent on naming fast cars, airplanes or trains, he thought. Borges, famously, stopped being an *ultraísta* or avant-gardist after writing his first *ultraísta* poem, a witty friend, Néstor Ibarra, noted. In keeping with his bookish sensibility, Borges developed a reflective, intimate way of writing, with 'laconic metaphors', as he put it. In his memoirs he would say that he had never strayed beyond that first book of poems: 'I feel that all during my lifetime I have been rewriting that one book.'[7]

Borges has created a legend out of how he distributed this first book *Fervor de Buenos Aires*, paid for by his father. It was rushed into print because the Borges family had to return to Europe for another eye operation on his father (they left in July 1923 and stayed for a year). He had written 64 poems, but had to drop six because they didn't fit into the pagination. No proof-reading, no table of contents, no page numbers and cheap paper. In a hasty, amateurish way 300 copies were printed. To get rid of copies, Borges modestly inserted them into coats hanging in the hall of his publisher Alfredo Bianchi, rather than handing them out face to face. People would be forced to read these free books. Soon after this incident the Borges family sailed off again to Europe.

Borges had arrived home in 1921 as a leader of the young rebels; however, he opposed the dominant French influence of Dada and

Surrealism, that 'Frenchified sect of voices . . . gesticulating babbles' (*balbuceos*).[8] He hated the French idea of literary groups self-publicizing themselves. Borges also turned on the previous Latin American poets who gathered together under the banner of striving to be modern and cosmopolitan, the *modernistas*, especially the imitators of Nicaraguan Rubén Darío, who had lived in Buenos Aires from 1893 to 1898. Darío was leader of an exaggerated, clever, over-cultured mode of writing. Borges claimed that 'simulacra of Rubén infected the presses'.[9] His antipathy pushed him to write about local realities and direct experiences. He also picked on the most revered poet in Argentina at the time, Leopoldo Lugones (1874–1938), and his towering influence over second-rate writers, that 'vigente lugonería' ('current Lugonese', Borges's neologism). Lugones would become Director of the Biblioteca del Maestro, and Borges would later confess that his generation's preference for the metaphor above all else in fact derived from Lugones; that they had discovered the metaphors that Lugones had already aired in his outrageous *Lunario sentimental* (1906). Lugones never publicly alluded to Borges, but bore him in mind when he attacked the avant-gardists as a mixture from 'overseas' (*de ultramar*), creating fraudulent, metre-less verse based on ugliness and 'sterility'.[10] It was an early xenophobic reaction to Borges's cosmopolitanism. What is clear from Borges's experience is that he quickly rid himself of any avant-garde tics. Instead. a poetic honesty guided him to writing more intimate, speculative and intellectual poems. Borges had never swallowed the revolutionary and political ambitions of the European avant-garde; he was always interested in poetry, 'arte pura'. He mocked his earlier baroque ambitions in a poem dedicated to the seventeenth-century Spanish poet Baltasar Gracián. He claimed that 'I am the Gracián of that poem', moaning about his 'labyrinths, puns, emblems / Frozen and laborious nothings . . . There was no poetry in his soul, only a vain / herbarium of metaphors and sophistry' (that is, ideas came before music). In

1937 Borges looked back and blamed his *ultraísta* phase as insincere and false.[11] He related this naïve attitude to his timidity, hiding inner poverty behind 'noisy novelties'. Poetry has to be sincere, deal with each individual's 'íntima pobreza' ('intimate poverty'), those nine or ten personal words that express what he feels. This Franciscan poverty of experience is linked simply to the limitations of being an individual with limited experiences. Poetry, Borges later said to Cortínez, was 'the only sincere thing in me'.[12] If poetry is a confidence addressed to a reader, its premise must be the 'veracity of he who speaks'. Reading Borges's poetry, then, is a direct route into his innerness, his soul.

Borges also brought back home with him from Madrid and Seville an ideal of the literary life based on avant-garde group activities, which resolved the problems of solitary writing and reading. Borges had no job; he read, reviewed, strolled and chatted all day long. Literary friendships and love-crushes filled his days and nights. There is a typical *porteño* note about always being in a group, in cafés, talking. It is based on an oral culture, where learning must shine in chit-chat and wit, derived from the Spanish ritual of *tertulias*. He called this the 'art of disagreeing', and his vocabulary is replete with argumentative verbs like 'refute', 'contradict', 'postulate'. He wrote: 'I'm intelligent with intelligent people and a nullity with thick ones, like everybody else.'[13] So he aimed at the challenging ones. He confessed to a cult of friendship, and none was more stimulating than his father's odd friend Macedonio Fernández, the 'major event of my return' wrote Borges.[14] Macedonio Fernández (1874–1952), 25 years his senior, was a widower, a Socratic man who lived in boarding houses in Tribunales, strummed the guitar, meditated and spent hours in cafés and bars, an 'outstanding conversationalist', but prone to bouts of silence. In a letter to Ramón Gómez de la Serna, Macedonio described himself as weighing 53 kilos, without an ounce of fat, covered in layers of clothes because he was always cold, a blue-eyed widower who

wanted to be a mystic.[15] He wore a black bowler hat, had long grey
hair, never undressed to go to bed, wrapped a towel round his head
to fend off drafts, hated dentists, fell in love with passing whores
and was a joker and a nationalist. However, his written works do
not catch the man Borges revered, his guru, 'the real Macedonio
was in his conversation', wrote Borges. A hostile poet, Pedro Juan
Vignale, mocked Borges as Macedonio's Plato.[16] Borges's brother-
in-law de Torre in 1928 lamented that this semi-genial frustrated
man had held such a diffuse influence on younger writers. Years
later in 1936 Macedonio joked that he was Borges's creation, that
Borges cited him to talk about himself and that he, Macedonio,
was the author of Borges's best work.[17]

A group would meet every Saturday at the Perla in the hum-
drum Plaza Once (a café with that name still exists there) and chat
until dawn. Norah Borges nicknamed them 'the Macedonians'.
Borges said that every time he thought of this plaza, one of the
ugliest in Buenos Aires, he felt thrilled.[18] What he appreciated in
this puritanical man was 'pure thinking'. He would arrive at the
cafés, pull scraps of paper out of his pockets, and say one or two
things in an hour. What he said was never affirmative, but threw a
dazzling light, Borges said, on whatever was being discussed.[19] Like
Borges, Macedonio would read a page or two and then drift into
pure speculation. Writing for Macedonio was simply a way of not
reading, a revenge on having read so much. Borges followed suit.
The real lesson Borges learnt from this natural philosopher was to
read sceptically, for Macedonio mocked systematic philosophy.
Truth was ineffable, incommunicable. Borges told an interviewer
that 'I started out by plagiarizing him devotedly'.[20] Macedonio
himself revered Gómez de la Serna, claimed that he and Chaplin
were the prodigies of the twentieth century. But for Borges, back
from Europe, Macedonio confirmed that eternal problems could be
aired in the here and now in a modest boarding-house in the *barrio*
of Tribunales. Macedonio could replace centuries of thinking and

all the kingdoms of Europe. Being was made present now, not over there in Paris. Borges shared Macedonio's jibes about venerable traditions. They once planned a jointly written novel to be called *El hombre que será presidente* (*The Man who would be President*). It would be a Dada gesture that would provoke a nervous breakdown in Buenos Aires and open the way for the arrival of Bolshevism, by introducing pens with nibs on both sides, sugar bowls that didn't release sugar ... But from this venture, Borges developed joint writing. In his funeral elegy in 1952 Borges said that happiness was having known Macedonio alive.[21] In a poem, he had confessed that he simply wanted to be Macedonio Fernández. This is the first example of how for Borges a living writer, a friend, was more than his works.

Equally crucial for Borges was Macedonio's nationalism. In the wake of this strong patriotism, Borges affected over the 1920s an exaggerated *criollo* ('Creole') stance. Creole refers here to white Spaniards who lived in the Spanish colony and had been born in the River Plate, in other words the original inhabitants of a Buenos Aires that was then a smugglers' backwater. Borges tried to be as Argentine as he could (due to his seven years abroad), copied down phrases from a dictionary of Argentinisms, dropped the final 'd' off words, changed the 'g' to 'j', the 'y' to 'i', even changed his name to 'Jorje'. He then seeded them into essays and poems that he would later refuse to republish. In a talk in London in 1964 he said 'I made the mistake of trying to be more Argentine than the Argentines.'[22] This creole patriotism was a feature of 1920s Argentine avant-garde writing. Lugones had rescued the protest poem *El gaucho Martín Fierro*, written in 1872 by José Hernández, followed by *La vuelta de Martín Fierro* (1879), as the epic of national identity, a gaucho outlaw as role model in the new immigrant Babel. A magazine, *Martín Fierro*, that Borges and his friends joined in 1924 was named after this gaucho, and Borges's generation has been labelled *martín-fierrista*. While Borges was away in Spain for a year in 1923/24,

Norah Lange.

a rival avant-gardist, Oliverio Girondo, wrote the manifesto for *Martín Fierro* in 1924 (as a wealthy landowning bohemian, he also backed the magazine). The whole manifesto is nationalistic; it attacks solemnity, formal manners and the Spanish past. It defends cultural eclecticism and sexual innuendo as Argentine. Over these years Borges ceded leadership to the extravert Girondo (and also, according to a recent biographer, the love of his life, Norah Lange, who fell for Girondo in 1926 at an event by the lake in Palermo Park).

In 1923 or 1924 Borges wrote a letter to Macedonio from Valencia, Spain and said that he would rather drop round than write, imagining the older man in his cabin on calle Rivadavia in Buenos Aires 'entre yerba, guitarra y metafisiqueo'.[23] These three terms define Borges's ideal of Argentineness: sipping bitter hierba maté (Jesuit's tea) in its gourd with a straw, hearing milongas on the guitar, and talking and mocking metaphysics. Macedonio left no written testament of his view of Borges apart from feeling that he had been invented. He did claim that Borges hid behind a 'picante idiosincracia' ('biting idiosyncracy'), reaffirming that irreverence underlying his work.[24]

The equally reserved and shy poet Carlos Mastronardi (1901–1976) Borges called 'my most intimate friend',[25] and shared with him 'the curious vice of discovering the city of Buenos Aires'. Mastronardi was from Gualeguay, Entre Ríos, and wrote about his humble provincial childhood of open skies and empty streets, close in spirit to Borges's suburban poems. No poet, Borges wrote, was more delicate with words, their emotional climate, their temperature.[26] He and Borges met at the Samet bookshop on the grand Avenida de Mayo in 1921. He was a bespectacled night-owl; a shy, ascetic bohemian who got up at sunset to start work as a journalist. He spent hours correcting his poems, hated spontaneous writing, wrote a study on Paul Valéry, and never adopted free-verse despite sharing avant-garde passions. In his nostalgic and detailed memoirs *Memorias de un provinciano* (1967), Mastronardi recalled his nocturnal street meanderings with his friend Borges. Once they found themselves outside the main vegetable market of the Abasto (now restored as a shopping mall), with the painter Xul Solar, who stopped to sniff rotting vegetables. They argued so loudly that a policeman approached and told them to be quiet. They involved the policeman in their debate. Borges laughed: 'Syllogisms with the police?' It then rained and Mastronardi opened his umbrella. Borges quipped 'You did well to open your duomo' and added 'It seems that rain only exists to fall on umbrellas'.[27] In the Munich bar on the Avenida de Mayo Borges asked the group's advice about poems sent to him from Mexico, and read them aloud. Months later Mastronardi recognized the same poems as Borges's own in *Luna de enfrente*. Another time, he and Borges wandered out past Nuñez and got lost in the dark in a swampy area. A policeman stopped them, warned them of the danger in this zone of thugs. They lied, saying they were journalists, but the policeman accompanied them back on to the lighted streets. In posthumous papers, Mastronardi recalled how in 1927, strolling into the *barrio* of Saavedra with its tin shacks, Borges said: 'If we lived here we'd turn to bombs. No other way out!'[28] Mastronardi recalled being invited back to eat dinner with the Borgeses on Avenida Quintana 222. By the front door grew a jasmine creeper and a fountain with a marble statue. A gramophone played tangos in the hall. They ate off old silver, on a mahogany table, surrounded by fading family portraits. Then they left for one of their long walks. Years later, the American poet Willis Barnstone evoked the quality of these walks and talks with an older, blind Borges: 'Rarely did a sentence pass his lips that should not have found itself on some page for the rest of us to savour'.[29] Borges gave numerous interviews, often repeating himself, but was always witty. Barnstone caught Borges's intensity exactly: he would 'plunge into talk about language and philosophy with no preliminary pleasantries whatsoever'.[30] This 'relentless literary chatter' is his trademark, his orality a sub-genre of the writings, but only recorded by friends like Mastronardi or later Barnstone. Mastronardi remembered Borges's acute jokes and Homeric guffaws.[31] Once, Borges dropped round while Mastronardi still slept to invite him out to celebrate the publication of the book of poems, *Luna de enfrente*. Mastronardi took ages to wake up. For months, Borges would joke that Mastronardi was in reality a ghost of himself. Borges always saw archetypes or symbols behind actual people, he added. Mastronardi would later become a close friend to the exiled Polish writer Witold Gombrowicz, enemy to Borges and his crowd. Borges confessed that he had never read Gombrowicz, but found the Polish aristocrat full of humour, marvellously snobbish. Mastronardi had become so infatuated with Gombrowicz that Borges forbade him naming him, so Mastronardi would refer to him as 'An exceptional man I know'.[32] Mastronardi, then, was a close friend, but they seldom saw each other.[33] In fact, Borges felt 'judged' by this loner of a friend.

Another friend was the painter and mystic Xul Solar (Alejandro Schulz Solari, 1887–1963), 'our William Blake', as Borges called him. Like Borges, Xul Solar spent his formative years in Europe, especially Italy, and returned home in 1924 after twelve years, with his friend the painter Emilio Pettoruti. They became the resident painters of the *Martín Fierro* group, exhibiting, with Norah Borges, in 1926 and illustrating the magazine. Like Borges, Xul is anti-realist, creating Klee-like alternative, inner realities, with much humour. He re-imagined a Buenos Aires with soul. Borges boasted that he had met three geniuses in his life, Cansinos Asséns,

Elvira de Alvear
and Xul Solar.

Xul Solar and friends
at table.

Macedonio Fernández and Xul Solar, the latter the only genuine
cosmopolitan, citizen of the universe. Amusingly, when Borges got
Xul to meet Macedonio Fernández, both geniuses in talk, Xul put
him down as just another *criollo*. Xul's inventiveness was legendary:
he redesigned chess, a piano, musical notation, new languages
and Tarot cards. 'He wanted to reform everything', said Borges.
He built up a wonderful library. Borges claimed: 'I haven't known
a more versatile and delightful library than his', exploring
Swedenborg and studying Blake's prophetic books together. In a
catalogue note to a 1949 exhibition, Borges conveyed his admiration for his friend: 'Xul Solar is one of the oddest happenings of
our period . . . His paintings are documents of an ultraworldy
world, of a metaphyiscal world in which the gods take the shape
of the imagination that has invented them.' Borges dedicated his
essays, *El tamaño de mi esperanza* (1926) to Xul, who provided five
little drawings that were excised from the posthumous edition
(it was one of the early books of essays that Borges had banned in
his lifetime). Borges would drop round to Xul's studio on Laprida
1212 (now a wonderful museum) and enter 'perhaps one of the best
libraries I've seen in my life'. A recent biography of Xul argues that
Borges's idealist world Tlön (from the 1940 story 'Tlön, Uqbar,
Orbis Terius') could only have been invented by Xul, and that the

story is a secret homage to his vivid and eclectic inventiveness.[34] In his memoirs Borges recalled asking Xul what he had done as it was a stifling afternoon (as it only can be in Buenos Aires in the summer). Xul answered: 'Nothing whatever, except for founding twelve religions after lunch.'[35] He remembered him as a tall, smiling man with high cheekbones, who lived a spiritual life.[36] Borges and Xul, similar to Macedonio, shared an aim to redefine Argentine nationalism; Xul's new language was even called *neo-criollo*, but in the 1940s their personal relationship soured as a more pernicious nationalism, Peronism, split them apart. Perhaps Borges's greatest homage to Xul Solar is the opening story of *The Aleph* titled 'The Immortal' where Homer becomes an immortal in the city with towers, incredible ladders and grey-skinned troglodytes, an incredible palace with circular rooms, clearly reflected by Xul in countless watercolours. Here they live in 'pure speculation', so absorbed in themselves that they hardly notice the physical world. They yearn for death, leaving as a sign of this other world nothing but words, all that remains of Homer's experiences.

Another intellectual friend, an autodidact like Borges, who in 1933 wrote the best analysis of the Argentine paradox, *Radiografía de la pampa* ('x-Ray of the Pampas'), and was a historian acute on local flaws, was Ezequiel Martínez Estrada (1895–1964). He was a famously grumpy character whom Borges considered a great poet and 'one of the most intelligent men I have known'.[37] He had the knack, Borges wrote, of making everyone hate him. Once Borges had praised him as the best poet of his generation, but Martínez Estrada interpreted this maliciously, avoided Borges and accused him of playing down his prose works. Borges, strangely, confessed to Osvaldo Ferrari that he owed most to Martínez Estrada's poetry;[38] that he was far better a poet than Lugones because his mind was 'intricate and very complicated',[39] though he has not survived as a poet. Martínez Estrada was on the fringes of the *Sur* group, worked in the post office all his life, and was a friend of the realist short story writer Horacio

Quiroga, bitingly described by Borges as having written the stories Kipling had already written. But Martínez Estrada and Borges shared a passion for the city of Buenos Aires and for the works of the pampas-born Anglo-American naturalist W. H. Hudson. When Borges once visited Martínez Estrada's house, he found it full of caged birds. In 1956 Martínez Estrada attacked Borges for praising the (so-called) Revolution that toppled Perón in 1955. He evoked Borges's 'encanallamiento' ('becoming a swine'), a 'turiferarios a sueldo' ('a salaried incense-carrier'), an expression that Borges in his public answer called a picturesque insult by an enemy who is a biblical self-dramatizing prophet, a 'sagrado energúmeno' ('sacred ogre').[40] Their public feud was definitive when Martínez Estrada later supported the 1959 Cuban revolution (and travelled there and wrote about it).

[canine]

Another friendship that ended in a public bust-up was with Leopoldo Marechal (1900–1970), who had begun in the local avant-garde as a poet with Borges, became nationalistic, then Catholic and finally a Peronist. Like Borges, he set out to study his city of Buenos Aires, which culminated in his 741-page novel *Adán Buenosayres* (1948). The novel, in its first edition, was dedicated 'To my "martinfierristas" comrades, alive or dead, each one who could have been the hero of this clean and enthusiastic story'. After the disturbing critical reception of this novel in the 1940s, he excised this dedication. At one level, the novel is a brilliant evocation of the 1920s, with long street rambles and discussions, with visits to the *orillas*, brothels and bedsits by the ascetic avant-gardists, who are easily discernible behind their pseudonyms. It drifts into satirical allegory, with a descent into Cacodelphia where Xul Solar (Schultze in the novel) functions as the Virgilian guide to the hell of Buenos Aires. No doubt that for Marechal, Xul Solar was the leader of this 1920s group.

?

Borges appears re-named as Pereda, a surname of one of the 25 leading landowning families in 1918 (and a joke on Borges's family no longer having any land). He is twice described as 'fortachón y bamboleante como un jabalí ciego' ('tough and unsteady like a blind boar'), capturing Borges's tough-guy physique (he had a podgy face and weighed 72 kilos then), as well as his myopic awkwardness. He is mocked as an absurdly folkloric defender of native *criollo* values (which even Borges reacted against). This Borges/Pereda had studied Greek at Oxford, literature at the Sorbonne and philosophy in Zurich, but dropped all that learning to plunge into gramophone (i.e. tango) 'criollismo'. Borges/Pereda ends up in the novel's underworld of a 'false Parnassus', accused of pretending to be a thug walking the streets singing badly learnt tangos aloud, caught up in 'fervores misticosuburbanos' ('mystical suburban-fervours'), an easy allusion to Borges's first book of poems, *Fervor de Buenos Aires*. Borges joins the group on their picaresque outing to the outskirts, takes part in lively arguments in the Amundsen family house (in reality the Lange family *tertulias* on calle Tronador); he's reduced to a 'criollósofo y gramático' ('criollo philosopher and grammarian').

After a nasty review of this original novel in *Sur* in 1948 by a collaborator and ex-avant-gardist called Eduardo González Lanuza (who accused him of coprophilia, excessive vanity, and being a Peronist), Marechal turned on Borges. In interviews, he belittled him as a 'literato' ('a man of letters'), a trivial 'mosaicist, prefabricating cocktails of ideas, following recipes that could be easily imitated'. In his fictional hoaxes, humanity had been shed for the sake of cleverness. Borges had become the 'enemy'.

Another key figure in 1920s Buenos Aires was the Peruvian poet Alberto Hidalgo (1897–1967). He had made a reputation for himself back in Arequipa and Lima as the local Futurist, famous for his loud poem celebrating Lenin. He moved to Buenos Aires in 1918. In 1925 he organized some sixteen Saturday meetings, often in the cellar of the Royal Keller bar on Corrientes 746 in what was the Comedia theatre, and called them the Revista Oral. Nothing was ever printed or written down. Writers, journalists and hangers-on would simply read aloud their bit through a megaphone, or mock or criticize their elders. It was noisy, competing with band music and other chatterboxes in the bar, and always chaotic. Such stress on the spoken word typified *porteño* bar-life. Filippo Marinetti, the Italian Futurist, joined in and read his performance-poem, 'Bombardamento di Adrianopoli' of 1912, though Hidalgo admired his slim wife more than him. Later in his diary, Marinetti alluded to Borges as timid, ironic, with thick glasses.[41] Borges was the defence lawyer in the literary trial, held in the Royal Keller, of Alberto Gerchunoff, the Russian-born Jewish writer who edited the cultural supplement of *La Nación* at the time. In 1926 Hidalgo managed to get Borges and the Chilean self-promoting poet Vicente Huidobro to join him to compile an anthology of the latest Latin American poetry, *Indice de la nueva poesía americana*, a 'bibliographic rarity' according to Emir Rodríguez Monegal. But in reality, Hidalgo did all the work choosing the 62 poets collected. Hidalgo was in the middle of the fuss over *ultraísmo*, writing a manifesto called *simplismo* in 1925, shrinking poetry down to daring metaphors and running a magazine called *Pulso, revista del arte de ahora*. He was alert, an extravert and a meglomaniac on a par with Dalí, blowing his own trumpet. Borges met him frequently, resented his self-centredness. He had a tiff over the actual poems that Hidalgo had included in the anthology, especially 'Rusia', his eulogy for the Russian revolution, for Borges by 1926 was ashamed of the poem's naïve political enthusiasm. Hidalgo specialized in insults. He accused Borges of borrowing money to drive a girl home and not paying him back. 'I'm sure that nothing happened in the cab. Nothing ever does between you and a woman.' Hidalgo also insulted the 'rich' who wrote, like Victoria Ocampo, and wished her a nervous breakdown caused by fellatio.[42] One of the acutest reviews that Borges ever wrote (his reviews are a sub-genre of his later fictions) was on Hidalgo's 1928 book of poems *Descripción del cielo* ('Description of

/Heaven

the Sky'). He opens with praise: Hidalgo is an extremely intelligent
man, but his poetry is a play on variations; his sentences begin
with previous sentences, not in feelings or life. The result can be
amazing, but usually enigmatic. This exclusively verbal invention
becomes a juggling-with-words, a rhetorical skill, a defect. Hidalgo
may have a cutting intelligence, and his variations may or may not
create effects on a reader.[43] Later, Borges evoked Hidalgo, the writer
– 'let's call him that', he added sarcastically in the prologue to his
poems *El otro, el mismo* (1964). Hidalgo had pointed out Borges's
habit of writing the same page twice, with minimal variations. Now
Borges laments telling this Hidalgo that he did the same, only the
first version was somebody else's. Borges justifies his sharp tongue:
'such were the deplorable manners of that period', and then accepts
that Hidalgo was right.[44]

Yet another key figure in 1920s Buenos Aires was the writer and
rich *estanciero* Ricardo Güiraldes (1886–1927). He was an experimental poet, close to his French writer friends Valery Larbaud and Jules
Supervielle (the latter was Uruguayan-born). He it was who gave
Borges his early copy of Joyce's *Ulysses*. He also wrote the best-selling
novel that closed off the gauchesque cycle, *Don Segundo Sombra*
(1926), when he himself was dying, published by Borges's *Proa*
press. Güiraldes's gaucho don Segundo Sombra was not only a
master in horse skills, but a guru imparting Buddhist insights.
Güiraldes practised meditation. After his death his wife Adelina
del Carril spent ten years in an ashram in Bengal. Borges met
him around 1924 or 1925 when Güiraldes helped him and friends
Brandán Caraffa and Pablo Rojas Paz launch their magazine *Proa*
(named after the dangerous and exciting prow of culture depicted in
Xul Solar's painting *Proa*). The first run of *Proa* lasted three issues
from August 1923 to July 1923; the second *Proa* would last for fifteen
numbers from 1924 to 1926. Güiraldes would often drop round to
the Borges house with his guitar. Borges once inspected his library
in La Porteña (now the Güiraldes museum) and evoked it as divided

Xul Solar's painting *Proa*, 1923.

into French and Belgian symbolist writers on one side and on the other tomes on theosophy, Madame Blavatsky, Hinduism etc., but all in French. Later Borges confessed that he could never finish Güiraldes's novel *Don Segundo Sombra*; this gives us an insight into how Borges read, for he rarely finished any novels (according to Boswell, Dr Johnson was also too impatient to ever finish a book). Borges captured Güiraldes as having a 'cortesía casi oriental' ('almost Eastern courtesy'). Through Güiraldes, Valery Larbaud reviewed Borges's first collection of essays, *Inquisiciones* (1925), essays later rejected by Borges, and heralded it as the freest and boldest work of criticism ever to come out of South America, with Buenos Aires as a more cosmopolitan city than any in Europe.[45] You could call this the beginning of Borges's consecration abroad, through his friend Güiraldes.

One last striking literary friend was the Mexican poet, critic and diplomat Alfonso Reyes (1889–1953), whom he met through Victoria Ocampo at her San Isidro *quinta*. He was one of the first people to take Borges seriously (who was so fond of jokes that he was seen as a joker). They would meet every Sunday from 1927 to 1930, and again from 1936 to 1937, in the residence on calle Posadas while Reyes was ambassador in Buenos Aires, and would chat for hours about Góngora, the Greeks, English literature. Reyes was a master of the apt quotation and understatement (virtues Borges paraded also). They loved literary gossip, anecdotes, enthusing about films seen. 'One of my best friends', wrote Borges. He had met his equal in unpredictable erudition. Borges once brought fellow poet Ricardo Molinari there, who thanked him by saying that the book-talk had given him 'the happiest night of his life'. In a note on Reyes's death in *Sur* (May/June 1960) Borges evoked the polymath's memory as virtually infinite, resulting in secret and remote affinities 'as if all that he'd heard or read was present in a kind of magic eternity', evident also when Borges chatted with him.[46] Reyes published Borges's third book of poems, *Cuaderno San*

Martín (1929) in his publishing house. However, Borges refused to collaborate in Reyes's magazine *Cuadernos del Plata* because Marechal, by then a nationalist, was a contributor. Reyes gave Borges the best advice he had been given: publish or you'll go on revising drafts for the rest of your life.[47] He also taught Borges that literary style was basically simplicity and directness.[48] Thanks to Reyes, Borges stripped his writing of local colour and baroque circumlocutions. Borges said of Reyes that he never locked himself up in his country (Mexico) and was open to the world.[49] Reyes, in return, called Borges a magician of ideas, and praised him for never becoming 'exquisite'.[50]

The 1920s, then, were Borges's heyday, when he met demanding, alert friends and argued all night, but this decade was also one of intense daily reading, usually in bed. A good example of the way he read was how in Buenos Aires he came across another master, James Joyce. He had heard about him from reading Valery Larbaud. Güiraldes passed him his copy because he couldn't read English. In 1925 Borges boasted in a review: 'I am the first Hispanic adventurer to have arrived at Joyce's book'. He confessed that he hadn't read all 700 pages of *Ulysses*, but did publish a translation of the last page of Molly Bloom's sexy, censured monologue in *Proa* (1925), with an Argentine-Spanish slant ('vos' instead of the Castillian 'tú'). Borges, as noted, tended not to finish novels; he found them tedious, packed with irrelevant detail and information. He practised reading 'retazos' ('snippets'). This thrill of reading something monstrous and new is in keeping with the daring 1920s Borges. Above all else, Joyce had captured a 'total reality', as if Mallarmé's dream that the whole world could end up in one book had been achieved by Joyce. Only perhaps Gómez de la Serna before had approached this total-izing success, said Borges, that presence of actual things. Joyce, he added, was a millionaire in words and styles. He was audacious like a *proa* (prow), the name he would give to his own magazine. Joyce, in his exile in Trieste, in his myopic dedication to writing, had

[handwritten margin note: Where the review was Published]

turned his beloved Dublin into the site of a new myth. Borges had hoped to do the same with Buenos Aires. He wrote in 1926 that 'there are no legends in this land and not one ghost walks our streets. That's our disgrace'.[51] In a later poem, 'Invocation to Joyce', Borges, now blind, thanked Joyce for redeeming his own petty avant-garde games, for Joyce had built his audacious labyrinth, with its splendid hells, with stubborn rigour, thus 'redeeming' Borges and his friends. Argentine avant-garde writing was tepid compared to Joyce. No academic distance in any of Borges's reading; in fact, a kind of transference, an identity reading. Borges became Joyce.

All his adult life Borges was involved in literary magazines. In Spain he collaborated on *Grecia, Cervantes* and *Ultra*. Back home he founded the mural magazine *Prisma*, then *Proa*. Later, he edited *Los Anales de Buenos Aires* and *Destiempo*. Over the 1920s he wrote for *Síntesis* and *Martín Fierro*, and became the resident genius of *Sur* from 1931 to the 1970s. Most of his work appeared first in these little magazines or in newspapers like *La Nación, La Prensa* and *Clarín*. You can define his readership as exactly those people, usually fellow writers, who read these literary magazines; he could count on their skills, knowledge and culture, and work his irony and in-jokes on a network of faces and names that he knew and admired.

Over the 1920s in Buenos Aires Borges was at the forefront of the battle for the new. When he returned a second time from Spain in July 1924 he joined in the fun centred on the magazine that would give his generation its name, *Martín Fierro*. It ran, in its second period (there was an earlier magazine with the same name) for 45 numbers, from 1 February 1924 to 15 November 1927. It was edited by Evar Méndez from an office in the smart street calle Florida in the centre Buenos Aires. It reached a large audience with its jokes and cartoons; number 18 ran to 20,000 copies. Borges was not the leader, though he joined in the japes

and tricks, and sat in on the banquets (with raviolis) in honour of
visitors like Supervielle or Ramón Gómez de la Serna, reviewed
his companions, wrote some satirical pieces. But he disliked the
way Oliverio Girondo, who penned the manifesto of 15 May 1924,
orientated the magazine towards France, taking sides in the culture wars. He scorned that 'bickering' and 'publicity', he wrote in
his memoirs.[52] In 1949 Oliverio Girondo wrote a history of the
magazine, read aloud at a reunion. He compared Buenos Aires
with Paris, which had Futurism, Dada and Surrealism, but in
Buenos Aires 'nothing was happening'.[53] The climate was mediocre;
the worst sentimental side of Rubén Darío was being imitated,
and 'celui qui ne comprend pas' (Remy de Gourmont's character
resurrected by Rubén Darío), dominated the universities, the
newspapers and cafés. Despite nearly one million inhabitants,
Buenos Aires did not have real galleries or publishing houses.
Even the national poet, Lugones, had to publish his own poetry,
and wait fifteen years to sell 500 copies. So the magazine should
be best defined as 'catching up on modernity'. There was a public
feud, invented later according to Borges by credulous university
professors, between the *Martín Fierro* writers and those, called
the *Boedo* group, congregated in bars and a publishing house in
a working class district. According to Girondo, it was Roberto
Mariani who called the posh writers, right-wing conservatives,
worshippers of Lugones (himself turning more and more into a
fascist), foreigners extolling fake *criollo* virtues. Borges felt he
belonged more to the *Boedo* group, as he admired Carriego, tangos,
the slums and thugs, but he couldn't escape his class origins, despite
being poor. Girondo called Borges an 'assiduous contributor',
though later Borges told Fernando Sorrentino that he was not really
part of the editorial group, that he had his own magazine *Proa* and
his own friends.[54] But Borges did write the spoof poem by Rudyard
Kipling called 'Saludo a Buenos Aires' in 1926. With hindsight,
Borges disliked his earlier 1920s self as 'priggish' and 'dogmatic'.

Over the 1920s Borges's love life, which I've called crushes, took on
its pattern. He would fall for a beautiful girl or woman, praise her
work in a review or a prologue; she would enjoy sharing mental life
with him, even collaborating on a book, but usually not move into
any kind of physical intimacy. When one of these Platonic affairs
broke up, Borges would speak ill of his ex-flame, what one of them,
a later biographer, María Esther Vázquez, would call his 'reiterated
scorn' for old loves.[55] His deep reserve concerning the women who
moved him meant also that love or women rarely become the topic
of his written work. It remains locked in his secretive mind, a
mental muse. Jean Pierre Bernès, the French editor of the Pléiade
Borges, the best scholarly edition of the work, knew Borges well
and said that he was always in love and always 'desgraciado en
amores' ('unlucky in love').[56]

In Marechal's novel *Adán Buenosayrres* there are vivid scenes in
a suburban house of a Norwegian widow and her beautiful daugh-
ters where the poets and painters gather, flirt and express their
daring opinions. This is thinly veiled, as I've noted, for the Lange
household in their villa Mazzini and garden on calle Tronador
1746. Norah Lange (1902–1976) (the 'h' was dropped in 1926) was
the sole woman poet of the *ultraísta* group, its muse. She was red-
haired and a teenager (fifteen years old) when she published her
first poems. In 1925 her first book, with its Borgesian title, *La calle
de la tarde* ('Afternoon street'), carried Borges's prologue and his sister
Norah Borges's cover. It was a family affair, as Borges's uncle had
married Lange's aunt. Borges remembered her house as bordering
the country, leading to his rediscovery of *las orillas* ('outskirts')
of Buenos Aires. Marechal called the place, with its lively women,
a 'philosophical brothel'. In a 1991 biography of Lange, Marechal's
accurate novel is used as the source for this period. Edwin
Williamson's meticulously researched biography has made Norah
Lange the great silenced love of a rejected Borges on the evidence
of interpreting poems and texts. Bioy Casares deemed Borges a

76

'very sentimental' man, and obviously 'being-in-love' loomed
large in his mind, but not with the same lover all his life. Another
friend also noted this sentimentality, although nobody else did,
she wrote, and Borges hid it well.[57]

But what matters is that Borges begun his string of love-crushes
in the Lange household, starting with Concepción Guerrero in
1922, and then, maybe, Norah Lange herself and later her sister
Haydée. But Norah sought him out as a friend and mentor, and
fell for Borges's rival, the rich, outrageous poet Oliverio Girondo
(1891–1967). In 1926 Borges reviewed Girondo's poems in the magazine *Martín Fierro*. Girondo scared him, he opined, made him feel
provincial. Girondo's work was violent. The poet stared hard at
things and suddenly knocked them over with a swipe of his hand.
His writing was visual and immediate. Borges doesn't add that it's
also provocative, sexist and macho, with women crossing their legs
in case their sexes drop to the ground, or girls from Flores with
phosphorescent nipples. It's an urban, libidinous poetry, summarized in the jocular, modern title *Veinte poemas para ser leídos en el
tranvía* ('Twenty Poems to Read in a Tram'). Girondo was a constant traveller to Paris, a close friend to Gómez de la Serna, a fine
painter who illustrated his own poems, a generous entertainer and
an exhibitionist always up to pranks. He finally married Norah
Lange in 1946. Earlier, in 1927, Norah had publicly criticized Borges
in a review in *Martín Fierro*. In this review she wrote that Borges
had turned Buenos Aires into one long quiet peaceful Sunday
(without life or noise).[58] She evidently disliked his bookish ways.

A close literary friend, the writer Adolfo Bioy Casares, once
noted that Borges was obsessed with Norah. Edwin Williamson
relates Borges's longest story, 'The Congress' (published separately
in 1971 and then in *El libro de arena* in 1975) to this envy of his rival
Girondo over Norah Lange. The story is about a club set up to
unite the world, where the narrator is charged with getting books
for the library from London, while a character called Fermín

Eguren goes to Paris. Eguren is a *criollo*, attracts women, visits expensive tailors, is a Basque and once revealed his cowardice when threatened by a thug. Eguren then hated the narrator for having witnessed his humiliation. Eguren's utopia was Paris, a continuation of calle Junín (a smart *barrio norte* street). The story is weak, slightly pointless, a shadow summary of his earlier fictions (as Néstor Ibarra decided), but Eguren is clearly Girondo and Borges did mock Girondo's poetry as plagiarizing *greguerías*. Interestingly, the secretary to the Club is a Norwegian with red hair called Nora Erfjord (in reality the surname of Norah Lange's Norwegian mother), though the narrator has a sexual fling with another woman in London called Beatriz. Does Borges's secret passion for Norah relate to Borges's classic story 'The Aleph'? This already-mentioned complex story also deals with an unconfessed love, with sexual failure and petty revenge revealed in the magical Aleph visions where amongst the myriad things glimpsed are obscene, detailed letters from Beatriz to her lover Daneri. Borges clearly concealed his failure in love to avoid public shame. But for me, the evidence of his naïve, sentimental side points to Estela Canto, a more likely source for Beatriz in 'The Aleph', as we'll see. Borges did admit to liking Norah's older sister Haydée, and dedicated the poem 'Llaneza' ('Plainness') from his first book *Fervor de Buenos Aires* about the calle Tronador meetings. It tells a story. A gate is opened that devoted routine has fixed in memory. The poet knows the customs of the house and the souls of its inhabitants. He loves the 'dialect of allusions', that sign of group intimacy that these Saturday meetings offered. He doesn't need to talk, nor claim privileges, 'bien me conocen quienes aquí me rodean / bien saben mis congojas y mi flaqueza' ('those who surround me know me well / they know my worries and weakness').[59] This is a new kind of family, with discussions of ideas and flirtations. Calling on the Langes was a high point in his life; to be natural and admitted in, to become part of reality, like stones or trees, that is, without inner

Borges in 1933.

torments. The title suggests a straightforwardness that must have been a deep relief for the uptight, shy Borges.

In 1966 Borges reflected on his *ultraísta* days, debunking the ideal of wanting to be modern when that's all you could be, rescuing German Expressionists like Becher and Klemm and perhaps Joyce's *Ulysses* from the wreck of the avant-garde. Argentina, late as usual, imported *ultraísta* ideas from Spain and repeated the metaphorical daring that Lugones had already achieved in 1909 with his *Lunario sentimental*. Borges even said that he should have belonged to the rival group of socialist and working-class writers in the 1920s named after busy Boedo street because of his interest in the city's low life. But above all, Borges shrunk his decade of experimentalism to talk: 'During memorable nights, we argued for ages over aesthetics: our work, good or bad, would come later.'[60] This Borges as a street and café poet gave rise to the legend that he was only really 'authentic' then in the 1920s, promoted by the socialist poet Raúl González Tuñón and other left-leaning writers.

What I take from the 1920s, when Borges lived an active street life in his beloved city, is an emphasis on male friendship as a particular Argentine passion, the 'deepest', the least public, he wrote. This often asserted insight reveals as much about Borges's dependency on this extended family as it does about Argentine social life. The best example of this friendship comes from tangos whose stories depict women as intruders and betrayers of this male ideal. This theme occurs in his story 'The Interloper', that opened Borges's return to fiction in *El informe de Brodie* (1970), for between 1953 and 1969 blindness prevented him writing stories. Typically, Borges first heard about it from a real friend he names, Santiago Dabove, and it's set in the 1890s in Turdera, concerning *orilleros* (tough men from the outskirts). The red-haired Nilsen brothers, with their family Bible, their slum house with 'zaguán', patios and adobe brick façade, were loners; they fought, got drunk, gambled, whored. One day, Cristián came home with a woman and his brother slowly fell in love with her too. They shared her, then decided to sell her to a brothel (Buenos Aires was then in the grip of the White Slavers). Neither thug could admit that both loved the same woman, humiliated by this competing love. After a while, they go back to the brothel and bring the woman home. Then they kill her, dump her body and hug each other. Male friendship wins out. After giving the first Borges lecture in London, in 1983, Borges was asked whether this was a story about homosexuality. He dismissed the questioner – a gentleman doesn't answer that kind of question. But Borges fed on male bonding in tangos, in the rough districts where men were tigers. Even the poem about the outlaw gaucho *Martín Fierro* that Borges revised several times as stories is, in the end, about friendship between two men, Fierro and Cruz.

The other level where male friendship permeates fiction is the closed circle of readers for whom Borges first wrote, many of them who lived the avant-garde of 1920s and 1930s Buenos Aires. In an interview of 1929 Borges said that he wrote poems for himself, that it was something private, but prose was for his 'contemporaries'.[61] A good example of how he involves his friends is the first story of *Ficciones*, 'Tlön, Uqbar, Orbis Tertius', written in 1940. It opens with Borges's close friend Bioy Casares, over dinner in a *quinta* (a house and garden on the outskirts), discussing the plot of a novel they might write together. Bioy tells him that he'd read that one of the heresiarchs in Uqbar said that mirrors and copulation are abominable because they multiply people. They try to check this in an encyclopaedia but cannot find Uqbar. Back in Buenos Aires, Bioy finds his quotation and brings the volume round. They discover that literature in Uqbar is fantastic, never relates to reality. They then try to check all this in the National Library, but to no avail. Another friend, Carlos Mastronardi, said he'd seen this bizarre encyclopaedia in a secondhand bookshop on Corrientes and Talcahuano. Further actual friends enter the debate in this story, Néstor Ibarra, Borges's first translator into French, Ezequiel Martínez Estrada, Drieu La Rochelle, the Mexican polymath and ambassador Alfonso Reyes, Xul Solar and Enrique Amorim (all introduced in this biography). These male friends become his ideal readers, a club of exceptionally erudite and witty companions, a dreamed-of café *tertulia*, where they share this mocking of erudition and idealism. They are the implicit destinees of Borges's fictions. He claimed later that 'friendship is the one redeeming Argentine passion'.[62] This inner circle fosters that sense, for later readers, of being outside, excluded, not in on the private jokes. It is the source of the cult reader of Borges, before he became famous. Asked by Ronald Christ about his ideal audience, Borges replied 'a few personal friends of mine'.[63]

4

The 1930s, Crisis and Accident

Borges turned his back on much that he had written in the 1920s.
He had published three books of poems, *Fervor de Buenos Aires*
(1923), *Luna de enfrente* (1925) and *Cuaderno San Martín* (1929). For
the last one he even won the second prize for poetry for the City of
Buenos Aires, worth 3,000 pesos. He famously went out and bought
the eleventh 1910/11 edition of the *Encyclopaedia Britannica* (all 29
volumes), the source of much of his erudition and of his style. Over
the years, he has tidied up many of the poems, sign of inner dissatisfaction, especially excising his spurious Argentineness and all avant-
garde traces. He also published three books of reviews and essays,
Inquisiciones (1925), *El tamaño de mi esperanza* (1926) and *El idioma
de los argentinos* (1928), all of which he refused to republish in his
lifetime, what Jean-Pierre Bernès called his Quixotic auto-da-fe, and
in 1930 his biography *Evaristo Carriego*. Seven books in seven years.
Yet he felt a failure, that he'd taken the wrong tack, and was sick-
ened by his avant-garde leanings as much as by his folksy *criollo*
postures, 'sham local colour' in his words. Borges wrote later in
1970: 'This period, from 1921 to 1930, was one of great activity,
but much of it was perhaps reckless and even pointless.'[1]

Borges was not immune to events like the Great Wall Street
Crash of 1929, that wrecked the Argentine economy, or the rise
of Nazi and fascist parties in Europe and their reverberations in
Argentina. The fun was taken out of literary life. Borges reacted to
events by becoming a supporter of the Radical party's political boss

awk

Hipólito Yrigoyen, known by everybody as El Peludo (a kind of armadillo that buries itself in its burrow) in his re-election to the presidency in 1928, though an old man of 78 years. In 1927 Borges was the president of the Comité Yrigoyenista de Intelectuales Jóvenes, with his companion (and later enemy) Leopoldo Marechal as Vice President and friends like Carlos Mastronardi co-signing. When the military led a coup to get rid of Yrigoyen in 1930, what has been called the Infamous Decade set in, with the army and the right-wing in charge, justifying their seizure of power with obviously corrupt elections. So Borges was, surprisingly, a Radical, the party that represented the middle classes and immigrants (he didn't join the Conservative Party until much later in 1963 and soon left). It was over Yrigoyen's re-election that Evar Méndez, the editor, had to close the magazine *Martín Fierro*. In an open letter, probably drafted by Borges (according to Edwin Williamson) and published in the daily *Crítica* on 4 January 1928, six reasons are listed for leaving the magazine, including rejecting the now dated avant-garde (enough allusions to gramophones, motorcars) and 'all that junk'.[2] Borges dictated another letter while recovering from a cataract operation on 24 March 1928, where he explained that he supported the Spartan Yrigoyen because he represented 'Argentine continuity', was a *porteño* gent and lived in a modest house on calle Garay (a talismanic street referred to in the stories 'The South' and 'The Aleph').

Nevertheless, a political setback cannot explain his retreat from this livelier self into what amounts to depression. According to a biographer, he twice tried to commit suicide in 1934, the lowest point in his life, due to general state of love-sickness. María Esther Vázquez described how he bought a revolver and a bottle of gin and went to his summer vacation Adrogué hotel, placed the pistol on his belly, drained the gin, but couldn't do it.[3] A later poem titled 'Adrogué' evokes the hotel's demolition and survival in the poet's memory, and ends, as if he Borges and the hotel share the same threat of death: 'yo, que soy tiempo y sangre y agonía' ('I, who am time, blood and agony').[4]

Something else that collapsed was his dream of repeating Whitman and Joyce, making of Buenos Aires what they had done with their Manhattan and Dublin, creating a new myth for the mythless city. For with his 1929 *Cuaderno San Martín*, Borges stopped publishing poems until *El hacedor* in 1960; that's 31 years without a new book of poems, though he did publish a collected book poems, *Poemas (1922–1943)*, in 1943, adding six new poems, but still a meagre output for three decades. Why such doubt about being a poet? Could a change in the city of Buenos Aires be a cause, a new consciousness of its dark side? The clue is the already-cited closing poem of *Cuaderno San Martín* named after a street, 'Paseo de Julio' (today's Leandro Alem), infamous for its bars, whores and brothels. The poem is topographically accurate, describing the *recovas* (arches) where you find 'prostitution covered by what seems most different, music'. As if music camouflages the sex-business. Of this street, Borges cries out, 'nunca te sentí patria' ('I never felt you as my fatherland'). In the poem, this foreign street conveys his disgust in a string of nouns and adjectives: a hell, deformed, a nightmare, ugly, perdition with its fauna of monsters. The poem ends: 'Your life pacts with death; / all happiness, just be existing, is adverse to you.'[5] He had excised an earlier ending which was more explicit: 'Paseo de Julio: heaven for those from hell' (that is, the thrill of sex for the citizens of a hellish Buenos Aires). Why did Borges yoke the impossibility of happiness with sex and vice? It was in the Paseo de Julio, as I've noted, that his female character Emma Zunz came to get herself raped by a Finnish sailor.

My guess is that Borges had now seen that Buenos Aires was also the capital of the White Slave Trade. In 1930 the national and nationalist poet Leopoldo Lugones had published a book *La grande Argentina* to refute the fact that Argentina was famous in the world for its whores's market. Evelyn Waugh, in *Decline and Fall* (1928)

85

and *Vile Bodies* (1930), has the character Lady Metroland interview girls for her brothels in Buenos Aires, run as the Latin American Entertainment Company. In his novels we learn that the League of Nations was after this 'procureuse'. Borges would have read Manuel Gálvez's bestsellers *Nacha Regules* (1919) and *Historia de arrabal* (1922), so close in title to Borges's fantasy suburban city, where the Genoese dockside quarter La Boca was 'the first market of human flesh in the world'. Tango and its slang *lunfardo* spilt out of this slum. This shameful trade was exposed by French journalist Albert Londres in *Le Chemin de Buenos Aires* in 1927. He snooped about, talking to the whores and pimps, to expose a network called the Zwi Migdal who met in a synagogue dressed as rabbis and controlled over 30,000 women forcibly brought out from Poland and Russia and often Jewish. A historian of this trade wrote 'The very name Buenos Aires caused many a European to shudder.'[6] This sordid social history lies hidden in the title of his poem 'Paseo de Julio'. Borges, as we saw, was a Romantic, a sentimentalist who believed in love but had an unfortunate brothel experience, and who has Emma Zunz call loveless copulation 'la cosa horrible' ('the horrid thing'). No document exists to confirm whether Borges had an actual experience that made him retreat into himself (Williamson claims it was his failure to win Norah Lange) or whether it was the city itself, suddenly a Babylon, packed with sex-starved male immigrants dancing the tango in queues for whores.

However, lovelessness was clearly to blame. Something about his own lumpy body made him aware that he was different. He suffered recurrent feelings of self-disgust. He had lived a prolonged adolescence of street and café freedom. Faced with having to make the next step beyond falling in love, that is sexually, panicked him. His large plump body was described as a wild boar and as a bear by Leopoldo Marechal in his satirical novel; Borges himself, on the back of a photo, called himself a 'wounded tapir', a Tupi word for a native South American nocturnal hoofed mammal.[7] Borges,

Haydée Lange and Borges in 1939, with Borges's self-mockery as a 'wounded tapir'.

Haydée Lange y Georgie d— tapir

wounded by love, retreated from his body into his mind and read all the more. The oddest self-image emerged later in a short piece called 'The House of Asterion', narrated by the Minotaur monster, half bull, half human, but stuck inside, alone and still. The psycho-analyst Julio Woscoboinik asserted that Borges was Asterión, autistic, introverted and solitary.[8] This creature felt unique and longed to be found and killed by Theseus. He won't fight and — *awf* wants to die, be liberated from himself. Borges had been inspired by a 1885 G. F. Watts painting of the Minotaur sadly looking out at the darkening world, first seen in a G. K. Chesterton piece. Strangely, Watts painted this figure provoked by an article on child prostitution in 1885, to embody male lust. This passive waiting for

George Frederick Watts's *The Minotaur*, 1885.

freedom from outside is how 'The South' ends, and how his grandfather supposedly died in battle. It's a secret wish behind the
fictions to be taken for who he is behind his body armour. Bodily
self-disgust lies at the core of a text 'Boletín de una noche' ('Night
Bulletin') of the mid 1920s, where he undresses to become that
'shameful beast, now inhuman and somehow estranged from itself
that is a naked being'.[9]

The dedication to what many critics consider to be Borges's first book of stories in 1935, *Historia universal de la infamia* ('A Universal History of Iniquity'), was first limited to the initials I. J. Nobody has worked out who the initials stand for. Edwin Williamson forces this into Norah Lange through Ingrid, the heroine of her travel book to Norway, and Julia, a woman two men fight over in one of Borges's later stories, but she was not English or 'innumerable' (perhaps a reference to Tennyson's 'Come Down, O Maid', a lovesong among the 'murmuring of innumerable bees'). Later in 1954 Borges changed his dedication to the initials S. D., who could have been Sara Diehl. The dedication in English is taken from the sole poems he wrote in English, titled 'Two English Poems'. In fact, it's odd that he didn't write more in English. When he published the actual poems in *El otro, el mismo* in 1964 (30 years later) he had changed the dedication a third time, now to Beatriz Biblioni Webster de Bullrich. But he'd dated the poems 1934. They are key inner documents that deal with *desamor* ('lack of love'), and penned by a *desdichado* ('unhappy man'). The first poem is directed to an unknown female reader (he clearly intended the same poem for different women), and is self-revealing. It emerges from a night spent chatting, but 'you' have forgotten the words and Borges is left alone 'in a deserted street corner of my city'. The second poem asks how Borges can catch this dark woman's attention. It's structured on a repetition of 'I offer'. But there is nothing Romantic about what he does offer: bitterness, his patriotic ancestors, his books, his loyalty, the 'kernel of myself' beyond words and time. Borges believes in some inner, wordless essence. The last long line is 'I can give you my loneliness, my darkness, the hunger of my heart; I am trying to bribe you with uncertainty, with danger, with defeat'.[10] The inner mirror reveals a bitter and proud man, as if defeat was in fact his sole reality.

were?

But there are countless further factors that combine to undermine Borges's street adventuring. In 1927 Borges had the first of eight operations on his myopic eyes. He knew that his glaucoma would inexorably lead to blindness. The threat of the gradual onset of blindness, of losing the visible world, cuts deep into his feelings from this first operation until his accident in 1938. In 1928, as noted, his close sister Norah married Guillermo de Torre and moved to Spain, abandoning Borges with his ageing parents. A poet friend Francisco López Merino (1904–1928), to whom Borges dedicated two poems, shot himself aged 24. A further factor could be that reviewing was taking over his life. He would later say that he remembered far more what he had read than what he had lived.[11] Too many hours reading in bed and writing his acerbic notes excluded life.

The 1930s, then, correspond to a darker period in Borges's life, where reading and reviewing take over his free time. In 1933 he became co-editor, with his friend Ulyses Petit de Murat, of the literary supplement of *Crítica* called *Revista Multicolor de los sábados* (his copious notes, commentaries and reviews posthumously published). It would be hard to calculate how many books he read and reread, building up his amazing memory of quotations, his idiosyncratic erudition. For example, he reviewed 208 books for the magazine *El hogar* between 1936 and 1939, and that's just one of the magazines he wrote for. Borges was a reader for whom pleasure was the guiding principle, whimsically not finishing books. Erudition and hoaxing went hand in hand; Borges loathed bibliographies, the pompous accumulation of sterile book-learning. The more he read, the more he took it out on his reading; writing, as he learnt from his mentor Macedonio Fernández, was his revenge on reading. About so much reading and reviewing in the 1930s, Borges later expressed amazement at such 'productivity'.[12] It led to the slow elaboration of his fictions. To write a hoax of a book review, to subvert book reviews with fiction masquerading as fact, were the prompts that he followed. In 1935 his *A Universal History of Iniquity*, which he called in the original prologue 'exercises in narrative

X Missing here is the fact he refused de Giovanni's repeated
requests to translate to English the stories, because
Borges was convinced that, if they appeared in English,
he would be accused of plagiarizing the 11th ed of the
Encyclopedia Britannica.
(In Rodriguez Monegal ?)

4 / 36 - 32
141

prose', derived from his rereading of Stevenson, Chesterton and
the eleventh edition of the *Encyclopaedia Britannica* that he dipped
into constantly. His source was a method he appropriated from
Marcel Schowb's *Vies imaginaires*, starting with real-life characters
and inventing new lives for them. Borges told Alex Zissman in 1972
that 'it was a kind of "half way house" between a hoax – a sort of
joke which I played on my readers – and a story'.[13] Borges's self-
awareness about his novelty was complete. His mock biographies
also emerged from his eccentric biography of Evaristo Carriego.
He felt that he was more the translator of others' tales, a reader.
Good readers, he warns us, are darker and rarer swans than good
authors. By 1935, then, Borges had inverted the Romantic relationship that we still believe in: the mystique of the author as the
embodiment of originality and inspiration, who Borges simply
calls a reader. His reversal takes on even greater effect today as
more and more people want to be writers and not to read. In 1946
he answered a questionnaire in *El Hogar* confirming that Argentines
prefer to write not read (and when they do read, pick foreign
works).[14] Borges is aware that reading comes after writing, that it's
more 'resigned, more civil, more intellectual'.[15] Here is the insight
into Borges's inner world; he is too lazy to bother to invent;
instead he's passive, rational and cool. In 1954 Borges penned a
second prologue and called this seed of a book 'the irresponsible
game of a shy man who did not dare write short stories and
whiled away his time falsifying and distorting other people's
stories, without any aesthetic justifications'.[16] You could call that
his revenge on lying in bed reading so much. So why did Borges
read so much? What does he mean by calling himself timid? We
return to his crisis and depression over love, poetry, politics and
his future. In 1954 he summarized himself as 'asaz desdichado'
('exceedingly unhappy'), and I recall Gérard de Nerval's sonnet
with its Spanish title 'El desdichado', which is about the Prince of
Aquitaine abolished in his tower and melancholic. Behind these

stories there is nothing, Borges added. They illustrate Buddhism's tenet, he wrote, that the universe is 'la vacuidad' ('emptiness').[17]

These baroque stories of 1935, as Borges would dismiss them, are culled from a bibliography of acknowledged sources at the end. ?
But some are invented. Indeed, as Norman Thomas di Giovanni has shown, one of his sources refers obliquely to his close friend the painter Xul Solar, who never wrote a book (he guest appears as Alexander Schulz, his real name). In these stories Borges originates what most characterizes his writing, his spurious erudition, according to di Giovanni. That is, he is erudite and simultaneously mocking of his erudition, so that humour and irony seep into everything. He also revels in lists, shrinking a life to a sentence or a scene, and avoiding psychology, as he states in the original prologue. This strange, stilted bookish book, *A Universal History of Iniquity*, also includes a story about local thugs (*guapos*) that sustains Borges's 'Argentineness', from the title, 'Man on Pink Corner', down to local details and words ('como si la soledá juera un corso' instead of 'soledad' [solitude] and 'fuera' [was], phonetic corruptions from the *criollo* outskirts).

Borges claimed that it took him six years, from 1927 to 1935, to write his first story 'Man on Pink Corner', partially to honour the Palermo boss Nicolás Paredes's death. He remembered slaving over every sentence, getting the voice exact. He wrote it during summer vacations in Adrogué, and in secret because his mother would not approve of this gangster theme. He published the first version in *Crítica* in 1934, where he reviewed under a pseudonym Francisco Bustos (a great-great grandfather). Borges would later also dismiss this first fictional experiment of 1935 as bogus, stagy and mannered.[18] He told an interviewer that it was a caricature, that concealing the identity of the murderer was unjustified, a trick.[19] He has a point.

This first story is a tribute to the toughs Borges had envied in Palermo. At this stage of his life, he was a film buff and wanted to make this story very visual. He has always thought that bookish pen-pushers were cowards, that real men tested themselves in wars and duels, the conventional envy of the sedentary man for the man of action, the real 'macho'. This studiously written tale then deals with manliness among thugs in a dance hall and brothel (*quilombo*) near the Maldonado stream in the north of the city. A man strides in and challenges another, who cowardly chucks his knife away and loses his woman to this challenger, who leaves with her. Then she returns without the winner, who has now been knifed to death, his corpse dumped in the stream. The narrator tells 'Borges', who is recording this story, that he had done it. Years later in 1970 Borges would write the version from the coward's point of view: 'The Story from Rosendo Juárez'. Borges's two stories confirm his fascination with slums and low-life, his unwavering envy of real men. More telling for me than a psychological reading is imagining Borges voicing his thugs as they dance the tango, repeating their way of talking, of dropping letters, using 'j' for 'f'. Borges, as he wrote and read what he'd written in secret, relived these dance-floor legends, the simmering violence, the readiness, or not, to strike with a knife, as if he'd been there reviving the obscure epic heroes of his childhood *barrio* Palermo. The first story is dedicated to his cousin-in-law and fellow writer Enrique Amorim, a reader who would appreciate Borges's careful touches.

In 1936 Borges published his fifth collection of essays, *Historia de la eternidad*, which sold only 37 copies; he'd now reached a nadir in terms of readers and prestige. Yet, this book contained a larval version of his later 'fictions', 'The Approach to Al-Mu'tasim', both a 'hoax' and a fake 'book-review'. Borges had invented an imaginary novel, named in the title and written by the invented Bombay lawyer Mir Bahadur Alí. So convincing was this hoax that the book was even ordered by a friend who took his joke literally. In this review Borges cited Philip Guedalla, respected English critic of the day, who had just visited Buenos Aires and written about it in his *Argentine Tango* (1932). Borges pretended that he had a copy of this novel, with its prologue by Dorothy Sayers, at hand. In his text, T. S. Eliot and Richard Church are cited. This fake review was written as an exorcism for so much reviewing, packing in plot summary, a mystical search prefigured in the *Mantiq al-Tayr* where the fabulous Simurg is each searcher. Borges carried this piece over as the first story of *El jardín de senderos que se bifurcan* ('The Garden of Forking Paths', 1941) and then into *Ficciones* (1944). In this hoax you hear Borges laughing. Luisa Valenzuela remembers hearing her mother Mercedes Levinson and Borges, writing a story together, laugh so loud that the laughter passed through the closed dining room doors.[20]

There were some compensations over this decade. In 1931 Victoria Ocampo launched the first number of her cosmopolitan literary magazine *Sur*. The title was given to her by Waldo Frank, and her models were the Parisian *Nouvelle Revue Française* and Ortega y Gasset's *Revista de Occidente* in Madrid. Borges wrote one of his quirky essays on the gaucho writer Ascasubi in the first number, and contributed to *Sur* throughout its long life, first as a monthly journal from 1935 to 1951 and then bimonthly (his stray pieces were collected in 1999). Through Victoria Ocampo, he would meet local writers like Pepe Bianco and Bioy Casares, who would become close literary friends, and visiting foreign writers like Henri Michaux, Tagore, Graham Greene, Roger Caillois and many others. It was also through *Sur* that Borges articulated his anti-Nazi and anti-Peronist position; he even wrote film reviews. Sur also became a publishing house. Its first book was Federico García Lorca's *Romancero gitano* in 1933 (Borges always mocked Lorca, feted when in Buenos Aires in 1933 for five months, as a gypsy exhibitionist), and Borges's own great fictions would follow in the 1940s. Sur, the publishing house, also commissioned his translations.

Sur framed Borges's life in crucial ways, thanks to Victoria Ocampo's insistence on meeting living writers. All the Argentine writers who wrote for her were defined by their anti-Peronism and

Group photo of *Sur*, with Borges standing, second from left. At the back, first on the right is Ramón Gómez de la Serna; next to him is Victoria Ocampo and next to her, Carlos Mastronardi. Sitting on the floor to the left, with a dark beard, is Oliverio Girondo.

support for the Allies during the war against Hitler. Looking at those local writers who were excluded from its pages you find Oliverio Girondo, who protected the younger Argentine Surrealists, Horacio Quiroga, who up to his suicide loathed luxury and the comfortable city life, Leopoldo Marechal, ostracized for his Peronism, Roberto Arlt, the genius of the poor immigrants, and socialists like the poet Raúl González Tuñón. As noted, the exiled Polish writer Witold Gombrowicz shared this dislike for the rich and conservative, a label which would cling to the *Sur* group for all its life. But Borges was not happy in this inner circle; Victoria Ocampo was too flashy, too snobbish. He never liked what she wrote, defining her importance as a spreader of culture (indeed, her main work was autobiographical rather than creative).

Jorge Luis Borges

Jorge Luis Borges

However, Borges met his most long-lasting literary friend through
Victoria Ocampo. The fifteen-years-younger Adolfo Bioy Casares
(1914–1999), who came from a wealthy land-owning family, was good
looking, a womanizer and a novelist, complimenting Borges's awkwardness, shyness and inability to write long fiction. Bioy had married the flamboyant poet and painter Silvina Ocampo (1903–1993),
youngest of the Ocampo sisters, in 1940, with Borges as their
witness. It was a peculiar and literary marriage, for both conducted
their respective love affairs with total freedom. The literary chats
and collaborations between the two men, and often the three with
Silvina, formed the backbone to Borges's 1930s and 1940s. The
routine was fixed early on. Borges would turn up to dine in Bioy
Casares's flat on the corner of Ecuador and Santa Fe, and then after
food they would retire and write. When Bioy moved to calle Posadas

1650, near the Recoleta cemetery, these evenings continued. Bioy
and Borges shared English gentlemanly values like discretion and
reticence, literary tastes like Wells, Stevenson and Kipling, and
a fascination for low-life (Rodríguez Monegal nicknamed them
'Biorges'). They collaborated on writing detective fiction and
compiled anthologies. According to María Esther Vázquez, their
relationship was not intimate or confessional but always literary.
Bioy had a string of women writer lovers (including Octavio Paz's
first wife Elena Garro in Paris), but was a gentleman who surely
never boasted. Despite this, Borges lived vicariously through his
friend's worldliness.

They first met at Victoria Ocampo's grand riverbank house at
San Isidro in 1932. Bioy was 18 and Borges 33. Bioy admitted liking
Borges's essays, but not the poems. He later summed Borges up as
'very intelligent, an *enfant terrible*' and viewed him as a 'paradoxical'
man, a heretic. Bioy never could penetrate Borges's reserve,
and guessed that deep down he was 'very sentimental'. Through
swapping after-dinner plots with Bioy, Borges became a short story
writer. Their first literary collaboration was around 1935 or 1936 in
an uncle of Bioy's *estancia* (called the Rincón Viejo) in Pardo. It was
cold, the house was falling down and they sat in front of a fire in
the dining room and wrote a well-paid jointly written but anonymous advertising leaflet on the merits of La Martona yoghurt,
with recipes. They then collaborated with anthologies, carrying out
most of the translations. They translated together very freely, with
no respect for the original. Fernando Sorrentino has shown how an
H. G. Wells piece for their anthology of fantastic literature was cut
down from 504 words to 220.[21] Over the years together, Bioy would
type out the agreed sentences. They adopted pseudonyms for their
detective writing. Borges chose Bustos Domecq and Bioy, Suárez
Lynch (both old family names). Borges is fascinating when describing how they worked together, defying anyone to say who wrote
what because they created a third entity, unlike either of them,

more humorous, 'as if the teller hardly understood what he was saying'.[22] The secret, he felt, was that he and Bioy were never rivals. Their first joint detective work, *Seis problemas para don Isidro Parodi*, appeared later with the Sur publishing house in 1942. They had intended to write serious detective stories for the newspaper *La Nación*, but their collaboration turned into farce. Their friends had objected to this kind of writing, but Bioy said 'we went on writing them because it was fun. We were always laughing.'[23] Their detective Parodi (typical immigrant surname from around Genoa) was falsely imprisoned in the Penitenciaría Nacional (since demolished). He was obese and around 40, drank *hierba mate*, was a bit deaf, a 'sedentary detective', who had been a barber in the *barrio sur* before being framed by the police. Borges wished that he had come from the *barrio sur*, from the working classes, and was always sedentary and plump, a mocking self-portrait. Each chapter was recounted to Parodi in his cell number 273 by a different person. He solved crimes in his head, like Poe's Auguste Dupin. All Borges and Bioy's detective works emerged from this first one. Parodi is close to parody, and all social classes are mocked. Such detailed verbal satire makes these collaborations almost impossible to convey in English. They completed many of the stories in Quequén, a once smart beach resort. This collaborative work of the 1940s is ironically close to the collective writing that the Surrealists attempted, an avant-garde lineage. From 1967, with *Crónicas de Bustos Domecq*, the two writers used their real names. In all, between 1942 and 1977, they wrote 39 texts of varying length and two film scripts. In 1936 they founded a literary review tellingly titled *Destiempo* ('Out of Time') with three numbers. Borges, Bioy once said, never gave into convention, idleness or snobbery and had an inexhaustible inventive energy. He also gave good advice: don't edit books or magazines, just read and write. It's telling that they only collaborated over spoofs, no joint poems or essays (in these genres Borges remained serious and often sincere). However,

The last photo of Borges and Adolfo Bioy Casares together in 1986, taken in Casares's bookshop on calle Suipacha.

satire crept into Borges's fictions, especially in 'Pierre Menard' and 'The Aleph'. Later, Bioy claimed that one evening with Borges was the equivalent of years of solitary writing, so collaboration was his writer's school.

In 1936 the Belgian poet and later painter Henri Michaux (1899–1984) was invited by Victoria Ocampo to Buenos Aires to give a lecture on the topic of the quest in contemporary French poetry (the sole time that he ever spoke as a critic). She had been alerted to him by the poet Jules Supervielle, and he'd been translated by Guillermo de Torre in the sixth number of *Sur* in 1932. Michaux left France as part of a delegation to the fourteenth PEN club meeting, held in Buenos Aires. He travelled with the fascist-Futurist poet

Marinetti, with Ungaretti and with his Uruguayan-born friend Jules Supervielle, and stayed for five months (until January 1937). In Uruguay, Michaux fell in love with a literary lady, Susana Soca, and then with Angélica, another of Victoria Ocampo's younger sisters, but was rejected. He also met Borges, who would become his translator; they talked during long rambles round the city. Michaux knew Spanish after his earlier thirteen-month trip to Ecuador from 1927 to 1929, published as *Ecuador* (1929).

Jorge Luis Borges translated Henri Michaux's eccentric travel book *Un barbare en Asie* (1933) into Spanish in 1941 for *Sur*. It was not a task, he wrote in the prologue, but fun. Borges had published a poem alongside Michaux in April 1931 in the sole number of *Imán*, an avant-garde magazine funded by a rich Argentine Elvira de Alvear and edited by the Cuban writer and musicologist Alejo Carpentier in Paris (also included were Jean-Paul Sartre and Xul Solar). Borges wrote a poem about her that is engraved on a plaque of her family vault in the Recoleta cemetery;[24] in another poem titled 'Buenos Aires' he remembered her careful writer's notebook that became indecipherable as she slipped into dementia. He was in love with her; rumour has it that she was another candidate for the person behind the character Beatriz Viterbo in 'The Aleph', another woman who jilted him. That makes her the third candidate, with Norah Lange and Estela Canto, proof of how hard it is to pin a literary character to a real life one.

Borges met Michaux in 1936 in Buenos Aires. According to Borges, he was severe, smiley, extremely lucid, and ironic, and didn't believe in Paris, literary groups, Picasso or in Parisian versions of Eastern wisdom (today's Orientalism). He adored Paul Klee's work. These opinions were obviously close to Borges's. Borges's most acclaimed parable, his already-cited 'Borges and I', was probably written in the 1940s. It is his tribute to Michaux's earlier dramatizing of the selves in conflict in prose works such as *Mes propriétés* (1927) and *Un certain plume* (1930). Which is the real self and who is the real Borges? The famous one who has written all the stories and essays, who has won prizes and lectures around the world, or the other one who likes the taste of coffee, is modest, almost anonymous? Of course, both are the authors, writing is their battle, their confrontation, and comes from this inner space – Michaux's term – which is empty. No biographers have followed up this meeting between Michaux and Borges, or seen the parallels: the distaste for Surrealism, the fascination with Buddhism, the inner world, literary games, subverting realism. Both admired Chesterton and Gómez de la Serna. In a note on Jules Supervielle, Borges disinterred that Parisian sectarian literary life that both he and Michaux deplored.[25]

Over the bleak 1930s, despite a new set of literary friends, Borges also suffered family losses. His beloved English grandmother, who lived with him at home on Pueyrredón 2190, died in 1935. In a poem, 'Variación' (1970), Borges referred to her, without naming her, when on the point of dying she swore 'carajo, let me die in peace' for the first time in her life (like Ursula in Gabriel García Márquez's *Hundred Years of Solitude*, who finally swore after reaching her century). Then his father died on 24 February 1938. Ironically, in 1935 an eye operation had restored his sight for his remaining three years. Borges barely alludes to this death, his grief far too private for words, though he was there. Apparently, his father died by refusing food and medicine, a passive suicide. Borges told Sábato in 1975 that he approved of suicide.[26] Because of his father's failing health Borges had had to get his first job in 1937, at the age of 38. Through contacts, Borges was appointed first assistant in the Miguel Cané public library in the distant working-class area of Almagro Sur on Carlos Calvo 4319. He was paid 210 pesos a month, which rose to 240 (about US $80 today) for six hours work a day. There were 53 employees, and the Catholic poet Francisco Luis Bernárdez, once a friend and fellow *Ultraísta*, was the overall director of municipal libraries. He was asked to classify the books, and worked at such a rate that his fellow librarians complained that he would get them sacked as there would be no further work to do, so Borges slowed down to 40 books a day. He hated his colleagues, who chatted about football and sex (a woman was even raped there). Another librarian noticed that they had a book by a person with the same name as Borges, with not the slightest idea that he was the very same poet. The rest of his nine years at this library he simply carried on reading, all Gibbon's *Decline and Fall* for example. The one-hour journey on the number 7 tram there and back was where he reread all Dante in Carlyle's brother's English translation, and also learnt Italian (he first wrote about Dante in 1932). In 1941 Borges would publish what he called his Kafkan story 'The Library of Babel', collected in *Ficciones*, one of his most renowned nightmares, with Piranesi links between a library, a prison and the universe. A magnification, said Borges, of that municipal library.[27] The number of books and shelves in the story corresponded to the Miguel Cané's. He wrote the story while actually sitting in its basement; its source was a nightmare. Of course, all libraries have a mausoleum melancholy that comes from being trapped indoors, inside the mind. As Borges has often quipped, books are inert and dead until a reader opens one and reads. Borges often dreamed of action, of heroism. He could have written this story from having read George Gissing's *New Grub Street* (1893), where a character spots an official walking along the upper gallery of the British Library and 'likened him to a black, lost soul doomed to wander in an eternity of vain research along endless shelves'. In 'The Library of Babel' there are no women, no windows, no luxuries, no privacy, no home – just endless unreadable books on shelves, mirrors and dumb librarians. A parable about loneliness and despair, with its writing a kind of self-therapy or exorcism.[28] Within this dark, dystopic story of countless unreadable books, written in unimaginable languages or codes, one line had made sense out of the random combination of letters, a teasing pre-Socratic snippet: 'Oh tiempo tus pirámides' ('Oh Time your pyramids'),[29] and you can hear Borges chuckle. First, he believes that only a few lines outlast all writers, polished by time and memory into aphorisms. Time and temporality have also been Borges's own obsession, its nature, life's sure ending. Pyramids are human responses to time, a kind of funereal art. What only a careful reader will realize is that Borges has cited himself. His 1942 poem titled 'Del infierno y del cielo' ('Of Hell and Heaven') has the line 'ioh Tiempo! tus efímeras pirámides',[30] and his own line, the in-joke, is a paraphrase from Shakespeare's sonnet number 123 ('No! Time, thou shalt not boast that I do change: / Thy pyramids built up with newer might / To me are nothing novel, nothing strange'). A line from Shakespeare in the nightmare library is a felicitous summary of Western literature. Borges saw literature as the way we remember, or rather forget most of the works that we read to retain snippets, quotes, key lines. Every time Borges alludes to Yeats, for example, it's the same line: 'That dolphin-torn, that gong-tormented sea' (in fact, the last line of 'Byzantium'). We all reduce long, complicated texts to one-liners. Borges also wrote 'Tlön, Uqbar, Orbis Terius' and translated Virginia Woolf, Faulkner and Henri Michaux in his school exercise books in the Miguel Cané library. No wonder Borges could say of this period: 'I remember more what I read than what I lived.'[31]

The 1930s ended with an accident, septicaemia, a fever and almost death that ushered in Borges's most creative phase in the 1940s. It was Christmas Eve 1938 and very hot. Borges ran up some stairs to fetch a woman friend, Emita Risso Platero, who lived nearby on calle Ayacucho, for dinner, and cut himself with a casement window that was left open to dry after being recently painted. Borges hadn't noticed this window or possibly its latch (his poor eyesight to blame, and perhaps grief for his father's recent death or excitement in calling on the lady). For two weeks his mother never left his bedside. He suffered nightmares and much insomnia (did his insomnia begin with the accident?). Glass from the smashed windowpane was incrusted in his head and the wound wasn't properly cleaned. He lay between life and death for two weeks, delirious with fever, seeing animals come into his room through the door. Leonor Acevedo de Borges yielded to his pleas and read him a page from Ray Bradbury to see if he could understand, and he began writing his fantastic stories, which scared her.[32] His mother gave her version of this crucial accident in 1964 saying that something changed in his brain. Like Funes, his Uruguayan gaucho whose fall from a horse provoked his fabulous memory, Borges's head wound and brush with death stimulated him to write his great work. The scar left permanent bumps. Had Borges died then, as Harold Bloom noted, he would have remained a nobody.

The story 'The South' recreates this accident, but enriches it with meanings. The date is altered to February 1939, and Borges became Juan Dahlmann, who, though divided by discordant family trees, chose to die a Romantic death. He had got hold of a rare edition of Weil's *Arabian Nights*. Avid to examine this treasure, Dahlmann doesn't wait for the lift and runs up the stairs. Something 'brushes' his forehead, perhaps a bat or a bird. The edge or latch of a recently painted window had gashed Dahlmann and covered him with his own blood. The lure in the story to run fast upstairs was a marvellous book (and tellingly not a woman). Borges has written on the different versions (Lane, Burton) of the *Arabian Nights*, was fascinated by the endless stories, by Scheherazade's cunning skill in avoiding losing her head by telling a story all night. Could fiction postpone death? Does reading tap into another time-zone in the mind? Borges played with these enigmas in another story 'The Secret Miracle', where a poet is granted a year while waiting in front of a Nazi death squad in order to finish in his head a long play that otherwise would remain incomplete.

His fever and the illustrations from the *Arabian Nights* filled his nightmares. He was taken to a hospital on calle Ecuador (no hospital there, but it's where Bioy Casares lived), submitted to excruciating examinations. He was sick, wept and hated his body, his beard, his humiliation: 'minuciosamente se odió' ('he hated every inch of himself'),[33] a crucial clue to Borges's dissatisfaction with his physicality. Death by yearning to open a book was not the way that he had wanted to die, nor was death on the operating table. He had wanted a Romantic death. The rest of the story evokes the recovery. Over a coffee in a bar on calle Brasil (near the toppled president Yrigoyen's house, he writes), he encounters a huge cat that lives in the magic of the present and doesn't know it will die, and then takes a train journey south to his family's *estancia*. This puzzling cat stands out in the narrative and is distanced from the convalescing Dahlmann by a sheet of glass (the transparency of thinking). I call it Schopenhauer's cat, for whom the 'animal is the present incarnate. But precisely because this is so it appears in one respect to be truly sagacious compared with us, namely in its peaceful, untroubled enjoyment of the present.'[34] The cat is pure 'will', life force, health, what Dahlmann is seeking but cannot attain. Borges owned a fat white cat called Beppo. Dahlmann took the first volume of the *Arabian Nights* with him on the train from Constitución station as it was so linked to the accident, he writes, but he put Shahrazad (his spelling) and her superfluous miracles down, as he was just happy to be alive, like the cat. The train stops, and the story enters a dreamy finale ('wishful thinking' said Borges), where past and present fuse.[35] Dahlmann sits at a table reading his *Arabian Nights* 'as though to block out reality',[36] but reading cannot save him. He is confronted by a thug (one of those he loved writing about, but here in the country, a *gaucho*), is lent a knife by an old wizened gaucho, who like the cat, lived outside time (in literature) and steps out into the pampas. He would die now as a hero and not humiliated by a window latch. Easy to see how Borges twisted his experience to fit in with his obsessions about manliness, reading, time, eternity and heroism. The last brief paragraph shifts to the present tense of daydream and Borges postulates his ideal death, a man of action not a man of fiction.

5

The 1940s, War, Peronism and Writing

The decade following his 1938 Christmas Eve accident led to Borges's most fertile and extraordinary period. Up to the 1940s he was a poet who had rejected nearly all his critical writings, continued to write countless reviews and notes, but had not found a form to express his quirky, sceptical and *piquant* vision of life and mind. Over these years, Borges was supported by *Sur*, by his friendship with Adolfo Bioy Casares, by his caring mother, and in 1939 as the Spanish Republican cause crashed, his sister Norah and husband Guillermo de Torre who returned from Spain. It was a dark time and Borges continued to pretend to work and read in his Miguel Cané library. Years of 'solid unhappiness', he wrote.[1] I see a slow retreat into innerness, away from grappling with reality, partly because of his diminishing eyesight, partly a response to the depressing world of local politics and the Second World War in Europe. Borges would comment on all this obliquely, in parables. He edited an *Antología de la literatura fantástica* in 1940 with Adolfo Bioy Casares and Silvina Ocampo. This extreme version of literary fantasy was a relief in those foul times, and Borges was re-evaluating its position in the canon (as he would also do with detective stories in 1943 with his *Los mejores cuentos policiales*). He evoked these years in a review in 1940: 'I write this in July 1940. Every morning reality appears more like a nightmare. Only reading pages that do not even allude to reality is possible' (and he lists the cosmological fantasies of Olaf Stapledon, works on theology and metaphysics, the frivolous problems of Ellery Queen and Nicholas Blake). What developed as Borges's 'prodigious fertility as anthologist' (Alan Pauls) began in the 1940s, leading to over 30 jointly edited ventures, as well as editing detective stories with his Séptimo Círculo list.

To test if his accident had affected his mind and left him witless, Borges stumbled on a new kind of short story that compacted his book-reviewing and essays with the kind of stories Edgar Allan Poe wrote. The fiction that emerged from this testing is the wonderful 'Pierre Menard, Author of *Don Quixote*' and it began as a hoax review. When it first appeared in *Sur* nothing announced it as fiction; Borges deliberately avoided pigeon-holing it as a story.[2] A biographic reading would see it as a self-portrait of the artist at that crisis moment of 1939. The story bursts out loud with laughter and self-mocking. Borges told Luis Harss in 1966 that behind all his stories 'there's a joke'.[3] The list of Menard's published works reaches twenty minor publications, a forgettable, trivial bibliography of an over-sensitive, French provincial hack. That was Borges's severe judgement on himself. Notice Menard's mixture of pieces on philosophy and on poetry; on Leibniz, on Lull, on Valéry, as well as on chess and translation, with references to Bertrand Russell and Achilles and the Tortoise parable . . . all concerns of Borges's. Look up Menard in Gustave Lanson's 1923 illustrated history of French literature and you'll find a reference to Louis Menard in a footnote. Here was the seed. Borges saw himself as a footnote in world literature. He was a Menard. Lanson opines that Menard was 'too philosophic to be a poet and too much a poet to be a philosopher, more erudite than most poets and philosophers, with a mind encumbered with its own richness and burdened by its originality: he could not find the right form that would have placed him at the top which is where his fine intelligence should have got him.'[4] Here was Borges's dilemma: a philosophic mind that was too hedonistic to take systematic philosophy as anything but farce, and much too erudite to be the love poet he wanted to become. The story moves into absurdity when Menard decides to rewrite *Don Quixote* from scratch in 1918, soaking himself in Cervantes's world until we get to those two passages and are asked to appreciate Menard's identical version of three of Cervantes's lines because he, not Cervantes, wrote it. Menard's style is archaic, affected, typical of a Frenchman, while Cervantes was simply his colloquial self. Menard's futile exercise was simply an act of reading and translation, the kind Borges tried out to check his mental state. Borges's last joke is that most writers rewrite previous ones without knowing it. Menard knew it and still went ahead. To read the Quijote as if it was written by Menard, Borges ends his story, is no different to rereading the *Imitation of Christ* as if it was by James Joyce or Louis Ferdinand Céline. You can hear Borges guffawing in the Almagro Sur library basement. The eleven-page Menard manuscript of 1939 recently went on sale for us $500,000.

In 1939 Borges, his mother, sister and brother-in-law moved to calle Anchorena 1670 next door to where today his widow María Kodama runs her Fundación Internacional Jorge Luis Borges. Here Borges wrote 'The Circular Ruins', where everything, he wrote in the prologue, is 'unreal'. Its epigraph is from Lewis Carroll, equally unreal. Set in mythic time, it reveals a grey man arriving at a sacred centre in order to dream up a man. He practises and practises to create life from will power and mind. This is Borges's parable about creativity. He never liked analysing his gifts, would usually say that he received the story as a dream, and found that reading was a bit like dreaming, an inner experience only half tied to outer reality. Through different and improving dreams over a thousand and one nights, the foreign dreamer concocts his magical dream Adam, his beloved son who would not be devoured by fire. He would never know that he was in fact a ghost, dreamed up by someone else. When about to die in a circle of flames, the dreamer realises that he too was someone else's dream. Much has been made of this

story as a confession of Borges's debt to his father, but I prefer to
see it as a story about the wonders and frustrations of creating art,
with the awareness that there is no originality. We engender and
are engendered. Borges acknowledged the 'dim Eastern setting'
and that the title alluded to Pythagorean and Eastern cyclical time,
an archetype of the creator tricking himself into feeling unique.
But most telling is the trance from which this 1940 tale emerged:
'The whole story is about a dream, and, while writing it down, *extract from*
my everyday affairs – my job at the municipal library, going to
the movies, dining with friends – were like a dream. For the space
of that week, the one thing real to me was the story.'[5] I cannot
think of a better description of creative fire, or of being entranced
by reading. It is also anti-realistic; he has turned his back on 1940s
Buenos Aires, agonizing over Nazism.

Equally gripping was his story about insomnia, 'Funes, His
Memory', written in 1942. This absurdist tale is given extra pathos
if we see Borges's playing with memory as related to the threat of
blindness, a poet grabbing on to memories of a disappearing visual
world but instead being cursed by remembering everything, and
not being able to relax and sleep. The story is narrated by 'Borges' ①
who pronounces the sacred verb 'I remember' and tells of a young
and simple Uruguayan *orillero* (farm-worker), without a trace of
an Italian accent, around 1884 in Fray Bentos (near where Borges
would summer with his cousins). It's curious that Borges always
wrote 'Banda Oriental' (Western Bank) for Uruguay in the old-
fashioned way, as if Argentina and Uruguay were in reality the same
country on either side of the Río de la Plata. He felt he belonged to
both as Uruguay was his mother's native country. Borges remembers this man, he thinks, with his Indian face, his tough hands,
his voice, his sandals, his *bombachas* (gaucho trousers), holding an
obscure passion flower in his hand, but seeing it as nobody has
ever seen such a flower before. That is, Borges sees vaguely, myopi-
cally, with one or two details, while Funes, after his accident, sees

everything as it is as if for the first time, in total immediacy. The narrator, calling himself 'Borges', doubts more and more his verbal capacity to catch exact physical details. He meets Funes, who tells him that he was like Borges and all of us before his accident (he fell off a horse, unlike Borges who hit a window); he was blind, deaf, bewildered, a *desmemoriado* (someone who forgets more than he remembers). He was in a dream, forgetting nearly everything. This trance could be called the human condition. Even the words Funes exchanges with Borges cannot be reproduced, are irretrievable because Borges forgets them, isn't tape recording. But now Funes sees a present moment that's intolerably rich. When we see a glass of wine, he sees every grape on the vine, every star in the sky, a random unending list. 'My memory, sir', Funes told Borges, is like a 'vaciadero de basuras', a rubbish dump.[6] Just to think of something means he cannot get rid of the image. This rubbish dump with millions and millions of pointless images is both Funes's and Borges's, a wonderful metaphor for the unconscious when it cannot filter out useless information. Funes spent a day in a dark room trying to recover all the details of the day before; he tried to reduce his memories to some 70,000 images. He learnt Latin without understanding it. He couldn't conceive of the generic term 'dog', for a dog seen at 3.14 p.m. from the side could not have the same name as a dog seen at 3.40 p.m. from the front. This madness of particularities (Borges invokes Locke) in time meant that Funes couldn't think, was 'incapable of general, Platonic ideas'. Borges reaches this compelling insight: 'To think is to forget differences, it's to generalize, to abstract.' Thinking, inside the dark mind, with vague visual references is how he will cope with onrushing blindness. This wonderful tale is packed with further insights, but its biographical grounding is his fear of losing the world by going blind, and his technique for saving it in his mind through memory. In a piece on Joyce (*Sur*, February 1941), Borges summarizes his own short story in one page, makes Funes a precursor of Nietzsche's Zarathustra, a monster. Here's how Borges's mind works, a summary of a summary, a condensing and editing away of all but the necessary. Only a Funes, he joked, with total recall, would be able to read Joyce's *Ulysses* and remember it all. One of Borges's strongest, most Expressionist poems is titled 'Insomnia', written in 1936, and opening *El otro, el mismo* (1964). Vivid references to the lack of sleep, to not being able to distract his body, with nothing leaving his memory. 'I believe tonight in terrible immortality' he wrote. Borges was Funes all that night.

Equally dark and nightmarish, redolent of the war years, is his spoof on the detective stories he loved, 'Death and the Compass', also written in 1942. Borges preferred this as his title for the whole collection, but his publisher chose *Ficciones*. It's set in a dreamy Buenos Aires, partially in the infamous Paseo de Julio and then in a hotel in Adrogué, with its 'interminable' scent of eucalyptus trees (that 'interminable' is a typically odd Borgesian adjective; I'd have written 'pervasive'). Again, this non-visual tale is loaded with allusions to Jewish mysticism and books, but in essence it counter-points two ways of dealing with solving a murder, two detectives. One is called Treviranus, who is boringly commonsensical. The murder was to rob sapphires. No need to invent rabbinical explanations. 'No hay que buscarle tres pies al gato', he says in a wonderful, untranslatable, colloquial Spanish proverb ('Don't look for three feet on a cat', that is, 'Don't complicate things'). The other detective is called Lönnrot, with the word 'red' there to link him with the gangster Red Scharlach who set the bookish traps to wreak his vengeance on this thinking detective at the end of the story. His name is borrowed from an Elias Lönnrot, compiler of the *Kalevala*, the Finnish epic. Borges's Lönnrot is a 'pure reasoner', an Auguste Dupin (Poe's cerebral, sedentary detective never left his armchair), a gambler, a mental adventurer (almost Borges himself). Dupin was the father of the detective story, forerunner to Sherlock Holmes and Valéry's Monsieur Teste, Borges asserted in a note of July 1946: 'We ignore even his face: he has no other visible attributes but the infinite night and libraries,' as if he were almost blind, again like Borges himself. Lönnrot answers Treviranus's points by saying that they were not interesting. Hypotheses must be interesting. What he really means is that literature must be interesting, unlike life. So Lönnrot studies books, indifferent to the police investigation, like Borges reading during the Peronist 1940s. When Treviranus wants to talk about the murder, Lönnrott talks about the various names of God. When Treviranus interrogates a suspect, Lonnrött continues to peruse his book, with his hat on. This deliberate refusal to enter the everyday world is a self image of Borges, who chose to live in books (he never went shopping or did the laundry or cooked). But Lönnrot solved the riddle, with its symmetries of three, a map ripped out of a Baedeker (there was one once on Buenos Aires). So Lönnrot informs Treviranus where the fourth crime will take place, in an abandoned *quinta* across the polluted Riachuelo, south of the city. He'd solved the crime without moving off his bum, virtually; the actual circumstances, names, arrest, faces etc. 'hardly interested him'. He then falls into the mind-trap set by Red Scharlach. They meet in what had been Borges's summer holiday hotel Las Delicias and Scharlach recounts his agony after nearly dying from a police bullet. This agony echoes Borges's own fever, and near death of 1938.

Red Scharlach was trapped in a symmetrical labyrinth, with high fever. He hated his body, his two hands, his two lungs, as monstrous as two faces, like Dahlmann in 'The South' who also hated every inch of his body. We are back to Borges's own self-loathing. An Irish priest tried to convert Scharlach and he vowed revenge. He counted on knowing that Lönnrot was a 'pure reasoner'. At the end of the story, Lönnrot tries to wriggle out of being shot by the gangster by proposing another desperate labyrinth, a straight line, Zeno's paradox, as if unaware that he is about to die, but Scharlach will kill him again if there's a second chance.

Lönnrot is not Borges, just an aspect of him. Borges loved pure
reasoning, dispensed often with boring, everyday details, lived in
his mind, but, unlike Lönnrot, was sceptical of the mind's ability
to deal with fundamental enigmas like death or love. In his Pierre
Menard story we read that 'there is no intellectual exercise that
isn't ultimately useless'. The merging of Treviranus and Lönnrot is
the Janus that is Borges, mocking beloved philosophical doctrines.

The tale that captures best this futility is 'The Secret Miracle',
written in 1943. Set in Prague in March 1939, it concentrates on
a writer Jaromir Hladík, author of an unfinished tragedy, *The
Enemies*, and a book of essays, *Vindication of Eternity*, similar to
Borges's own *History of Eternity*, as the Third Reich's armoured divi-
sion sack the city and Hladík is arrested. In prison he anticipates
his death a thousand ways in his mind, knowing that reality doesn't
coincide with a desire to avoid it. To predict was not to postpone;
he was not Scheherazade. The pen-portrait that we are given of this
man of letters is wonderfully acute, another Borgesian self-mocking. He was 40, with a few friends, many habits and lived for the
'problematic exercise of literature'. He judged others by what they
produced and himself by what he planned in his mind. All his
published works left him with a 'complex regret'. This is so close
to Borges's assessment of his own work in the 1940s, before he
became famous. He lists his works about time, about Boehme and
Bradley, as well as his Expressionist poems collected in an anthology
and carried over into further ones, to the poet's confusion (like
Borges's avant-garde poem 'Rusia' in Alberto Hidalgo's 1926 anthology when he had discarded it). Borges identified with Hladík, could
have been Jewish in his distant Portuguese origins; the surname
Borges is common in Portugal and means 'bourgeois'. When the
Jews were expelled from Spain in 1492, they moved to Portugal
(or converted and thus set off the Inquisition), and then dispersed
to the New World and Africa, as Sephardim, speaking an ancient
form of *castellano*. Many were known as 'Portuguese', like the

Borges surname. We all have a drop of Jewish blood, he said another time. Borges was Hladík, identified with the fate of the Jews in Europe and in Argentina.

But Hladík, in prison, awaiting execution, wanted to complete his verse tragedy, and Borges gives us the details. He prays to God and dreams of a blind librarian also searching for God. He's handed an atlas with a map of India and hears a voice that his wish has been granted. As he is about to be shot, with a heavy raindrop running down his cheek, time suddenly stops. The raindrop freezes. He has one year. His only tool is memory (how these stories overlap; how memory becomes Borges's weapon against eyesight dimming). Hladík works away at his play, in his invisible inner mental labyrinth. Nothing can break his concentration. He finishes his play, the raindrop rolls down his cheek and he is shot. The real work of art, Borges implies with a laugh, is in the mind, in desire, an ideal, not in its completion. We all know that sour truth. Faced with inevitable death nobody will ever write it. This glimpse of an ideal that cannot be attained is the paradox at the core of Borges's 1940s work. Borges stretched this insight to define the experience of all art: 'this imminence of a revelation which does not occur is, perhaps, the aesthetic phenomenon.'[7]

In 1942 the Borgeses moved back to calle Quintana where they'd lived before, but to number 263, just off the Recoleta. Then mother and son moved in alone in 1944 to what was to become their home for the rest of her life, Maipú 994, where in all Borges would live for 40 years (a plaque now records this). From this flat he could glimpse the grand Plaza San Martín and its old shady acacias, tipas and jacaranda trees. In 1923 Borges published a poem named after this square and dedicated it to Macedonio Fernández, 'passionate spectator of Buenos Aires', this last phrase excised in later editions. To sit on a bench in the *plaza,* with the harbour below, was to feel the relief of absolution for this 'deep *plaza,* like a dream or like death', is 'igualadora de almas' ('leveller of souls'). These moves were all in the same area, the *barrio norte* and now depended on Borges earning the rent.

By 1941 Borges felt that he could publish the fictions written since his accident, and seven stories collected under the title *El jardín de senderos que se bifurcan* appeared in the Sur list, the most revolutionary book ever published in Argentina, possibly in Spanish. There's some confusion about dates, but the colophon in the first edition reads December 1941 (and the copyright 1942). It would reappear, with stories added, as *Ficciones* in 1944. It was entered for the Premio Nacional de Literatura in 1942, and didn't even make the top three. The jury's reasons were to do with politics, the narrow-minded nationalism that Borges was already attacking, and because the book was too cerebral, too dehumanized, initiating an ongoing clichéd critique of his fiction. The magazine *Sur* came to Borges's rescue, with a score of writers backing his experimental work in a 'Desagravio a Borges' ('Reparation for Borges') published in July 1942. A dinner was also organized in his support. Two years later, in 1944, a special prize, the Gran Premio de Honor de la Sociedad Argentina de Escritores (SADE), was awarded to Borges, the same year that *Ficciones* appeared. There was no doubt in their minds that Borges was now a leader, a figurehead, and as Horacio Salas pointed out, this riposte and secondary prize made Borges more known than if he had won the first prize.[8] The humiliation of not winning the prize surfaced in the title story 'The Aleph' when the absurdly pretentious poet and owner of the visionary Aleph under the staircase, Carlos Argentino Daneri, won the Second National Prize for Literature. A minor writer called Aita won the First (he was real, the Argentine rep for the PEN club) and Mario Bonfanti the third prize (he was a character invented by Borges and Bioy Casares, an insider joke, and was said to be based on his brother-in-law Guillermo de Torre). Borges, the narrator, added: 'incredibly my work *Los naipes del tahur* did not manage one vote. Once more incomprehension and envy triumphed!'[9] This book *Los naipes del tahur* was indeed a real book that Borges had suppressed. As well as being a mocking tale about mystical unity (the mystic cannot recreate his experience except in a random list), sexual envy and then destructive spite, 'The Aleph' explores literary envy, that competitive rancour that rules the literary world. Borges was nominated numerous times for the Nobel he never won.

However, in 1946, after nine years, and as a consequence of Perón's rise to power and popularity through elections, Borges was demoted from the Miguel Cané library to inspector of poultry, eggs and rabbits at a market on avenida Córdoba, because, Borges discovered, he had sided with the Allies in the war. This demotion was Perón's 'macho humiliation' of Borges, according to biographer Emir Rodríguez Monegal. Borges had turned into a politicized anti-Peronist. His position coincided with his defence of Western civilization against xenophobic nationalism. Perón, he wrote, 'was our vernacular imitation of fascism'.[10] In a jointly penned pastiche with Adolfo Bioy Casares titled 'La fiesta del Monstruo' ('Monster's Feast'), written in 1947 in the dense and untranslatable Buenos Aires slang called *lunfardo*, Borges alludes to Perón as the Monster. The story is narrated by a loyal Peronist thug to his Nelly and tells of a trip in a bus to a rally in the main square, the Plaza de Mayo, to hear the Monster speak. On the way, and already pissed, the gang (*barra*) bump into a weak, red-haired and absent-minded Jew who refuses to shout a Peronist slogan and is stoned to death. A nasty detail: the narrator finishes off the Jew by stabbing a penknife in what's left of his face. Perón and Hitler are linked as the Jew carries books. To both, bookish people are suspicious and are beaten to death by the *merza* (rabble) who support the demagogue. This piece was so 'dangerous' under Peronism that Borges could only circulate it in typescript. It was published in 1977, well after Perón's downfall.[11]

In a 1949 epilogue to the collection *The Aleph*, we read that nobody wanted Germany to be defeated more than he, but also that nobody felt the tragedy of German destiny more than he. His story 'Deutsches Requiem' (1946) explored this destiny that Argentine Germanophiles did not suspect 'as they know nothing about Germany'.[12] This is not a Zola *j'accuse* type of tale, rather it's a plea for separating Germany from Hitler. The epigraph is from Job, about relentless suffering. The first person narrator is Otto Dietrich zur Linde, a self-confessed Nazi about to be executed for his war crimes (the Nuremberg trials had just finished). During his trial Linde remains silent, now in this tale he will speak and wants to be understood. Two things ruled his life, music and metaphysics, or, more specifically, and closer to Borges himself, Brahms and Schopenhauer. (Much has been made of Borges's tin ear, but he wrote better listening to Brahms he said, and loved the blues and *milongas*.) Linde joined the Nazi party in 1929, and sacrificed his individuality to the cause, stripping away the old persona. He lost a leg, recovered in a hospital reading Schopenhauer, and learnt that all is prefigured, we even chose our unhappiness. He is appointed sub-Director of Tarnowitz concentration camp. Here he is faced with the Jewish poet David Jerusalem, once compared to Whitman, who loved the particularities of life with 'minucioso amor' ('meticulous love'). The Nazi knew his poems by heart, but drove the poet so mad that he killed himself. We're all born Aristotelian or Platonic, Borges insists, an 'eternal' antagonism. You are he, the hero is the traitor, the aggressor the victim. Germany is a mirror for our world, its hell. Borges walked a narrow wire illustrating Madame de Stael's *Tout comprendre c'est tout pardonner* ('To understand is to forgive'). He, like Linde, revered Schopenhauer, understood honour and heroism, and also that you don't chose your life and that there's an archetypal antagonism at play behind history. Is Borges an early post-Holocaust writer as one critic has suggested?[13] He had signed a pamphlet in August 1938 as part of a committee against Racism and anti-Semitism in Argentina and was a public anti-Nazi. Can his 1934 piece 'Yo, judío' ('Me, a Jew')

be seen as the start of his witnessing of the Nazi horror? This was
Borges's public answer to an anonymous nationalistic slur, published
in the magazine *Crisol* in 1934, that insulted him for concealing his
Jewish identity. The 1930s had seen the rise of an anti-left, anti-liberal,
pro-Catholic and 'patria' right that was as Anglophobic as it was
anti-Semitic: Borges's earlier 'patriotism' had been usurped by this
new Right. Borges, typically, opens with a notion that the past is
enriched by our ignorance; it's infinitely malleable and pleasing,
the chosen place for mythologies. Borges often played the game of
searching for ancestors; a sedentary and frugal activity that doesn't
harm anyone. His mother's surname once appeared in a list of
Judeo-Portuguese families, but Borges thinks he possibly derives
from a Catalan who arrived in Argentina in 1728. So why does
everybody single out Jewish roots, when they descend from a tiny
proportion of the world, why not Persian or Ottoman roots? Thus
he dismisses his persecutors with the charge of ignorance, and
stays proud to be a Jew as his title proclaims.[14] Not a shadow of
doubt, though, about Borges siding with the Allies in a pseudo-
neutral Argentina. In a non-fiction piece 'Anotación al 23 de agosto
de 1944' (referring to the liberation of Paris) he reverts to the 'enigmatic and notorious enthusiasm of many of Hitler's partisans'.[15]
Borges knew he couldn't question these Argentine sympathizers
themselves, as they were incoherent, didn't think they had to justify
themselves. He pinpointed their inconsistencies: they venerate the
German race but hate North American Anglo-Saxons; they're anti-
Semitic, but follow a religion of Hebrew origin; they idolize San
Martín (Argentina's liberator from Spain), but claim that South
American independence was a mistake. It was enough for these
local Nazis to chant 'I am Argentine'. Borges's flash of insight
came while reading George Bernard Shaw and recalling a local
Germanophile who burst into his house on 14 June 1940 when
Hitler occupied Paris. Borges felt *asco* ('nausea') and didn't grasp
what was really happening. Then, 'to be a Nazi . . . is a mental and

moral impossibility; it's unreal, uninhabitable. You can only die for it, lie for it, kill and spill blood for it.' Borges is aware of his risky opinion: '*Hitler wanted to be defeated*' (his italics). This strange insight about being released from the burden of self crops up again, here linking Hitler with Hercules. I do not see Borges as a proto-Holocaust writer, rather a propounder of lucidity. What the Nazis lacked emerged in a piece on Paul Valéry, written in 1945, about how the French poet and intellectual's personality is greater than his works. Valéry's (and Borges's) mission was to promote lucidity, a kind of heroism 'in a period of base romanticism, in the melancholic era of Nazism and dialectical materialism, with the promises of Freud's sect and the traders of Surrealism';[16] all mob movements restricting the individual. He was as anti-Marxism or anti-psychoanalysis (merely gossip) as he was anti-Hitler. His 1946 piece 'Nuestro pobre individualismo' ('Our Poor Individualism') puzzles out the meaning of local Nazism by attacking the idea of nationalism, of the left and right, as an evil taking over the individual's rights. And this would include Peronism. At a meal given in his honour after his sacking from the library, and published in *Sur* in August 1946, Borges incriminated Peronism, without naming it, as a dictatorship that fomented 'servilismo', 'crueldad' and 'idiotez' (servility, cruelty, idiocy); to fight this debased mentality in favour of 'individualism' is a writer's duty.[17] Borges, like his passive anarchist father, wanted a minimum of government and state interference. He often repeated Macedonio Fernández's dictum: 'More individuals, less state'. María Esther Vázquez saw this as the key to the real man: 'at bottom, a nostalgic and theoretical anarchist with too strong a sense of humour'.[18]

So Borges was sacked from his library post for political reasons. One biographer thought that Borges had been transferred to the School of Bee-keeping, but Borges's version sounds the more absurd. This shock demotion led to Borges becoming at age 47 a university lecturer in English and North American literature at the

Universidad de Buenos Aires (UBA) until he retired in 1968, though he went on lecturing the rest of life. He later boasted that he only ever failed two students. At first he lectured for the Asociación Argentina de Cultura Inglesa and for the Colegio Libre de Estudios Superiores and then all over the country on his favourite subjects, from Emerson to Dante, Swedenborg, Buddhism (noted at the start), the Kabballah, Cervantes and Icelandic Sagas. His prodigious memory, his passion for the subject matter and poor eyesight meant that most of these lectures were without notes. This oral Borges, with his fast, hoarse way of talking, became part of the public image (far easier to listen to Borges than to read him).

All the later 1940s Borges wrote and lectured under the threat of Perón, who had had Borges removed from the library in 1946. Perón, admirer of Mussolini, came into power with a coup in 1943, backed by the unions and the poor. By 1946 his power base was the urban proletariat, the *cabezas negras* (blackheads) and Evita's *descamisados* (shirtless ones). Borges, when he lost his library sinecure, was now a *Sur* writer, united behind the cosmopolitan group through their anti-Peronism. In 1948 Borges's mother Leonor and his sister Norah were arrested on calle Florida for insulting Evita and Perón, and then singing the National Anthem. They did have pamphlets on them objecting to changes in the constitution. They were condemned to a month in prison, commuted to house arrest for his 70-year-old mother. Norah whiled away her sentence in the San Miguel sketching the prostitutes and sleeping on the floor. Victoria Ocampo spent 26 days in the same prison in 1953, accused, with some thousand others, of plotting to bomb the Plaza de Mayo. The offices of her magazine *Sur* on calle Viamonte 494 were sacked by Peronist police. The upper-class Jockey Club on calle Florida was burnt down (and its fabled library and art collection partially destroyed). Minor incidents, perhaps, but vivid in the mind of the bookish, myopic Borges. As John King has argued, *Sur* took an 'ethical' position, defending democracy and civiliza-

Borges in 1949.

tion. Tellingly, *Sur* never referred to Evita or to her death in 1952.
In Borges's surprising story 'El simulacro' ('The Mountebank'), set
in 1952 (but published in 1960), a fake, Indian-looking Perón accepts
the condolences from the poor in that distant region called the
Chaco for his Evita, who is a blonde doll. In this shack by the river,
Perón is not Perón and Evita isn't Evita, but that doesn't matter to
the people. All her life, and afterlife, Evita was maligned by men
as 'esta yegua' ('that mare') as 'that woman', as having 'fellatio' lips
(Naipaul);[19] she invented her life and once embalmed, lived mind-
boggling adventures (narrated in *Santa Evita* by Tomás Eloy
Martínez). She was always fake, a doll, insinuates Borges. Peronism
is what people crave, a 'crass mythology', with nothing behind the
surface but fakery.[20] All his later life Borges refused to name Perón,
and Perón dismissed Borges as 'that poor blind old man'.

Now a figurehead, Borges was elected president of the Sociedad Argentina de Escritores in 1950, with its unfortunate acronym SADE, a bastion of anti-Peronism. It was housed on calle México, in the grand house that used to belong to Victoria Ocampo's family. It was a meeting place, offered prizes and stimulated reading. This was a crisis moment in its life as Perón banned foreign books, and supported demonstrators who shouted 'Alpargatas sí, libros no' ('Sandals yes, books, no'), part of a growing anti-intellectual movement that Borges equated with the rise of Nazism earlier in Europe. SADE was eventually closed down by Perón in 1953.

The *Sur* entourage had one further crucial contribution to make to Borges's reputation in the 1940s and that concerns Victoria Ocampo's much younger lover the French sociologist and critic Roger Caillois (1913–1978), stuck, like Gombrowicz, in Argentina during the war years. He had translated two Borges stories in 1944 (one was 'The Library of Babel') in the magazine Victoria Ocampo funded and that he edited in Buenos Aires called *Lettres françaises* (although Borges's 'The Approach to Al-Mu'tasim' had been translated into French by Ibarra as early as 1939). When Caillois returned to France in 1945, he worked for the publisher Gallimard and promoted Borges in French translation in a collection called La Croix du Sud. The French, as usual, were the first to spot Borges's genius. Néstor Ibarra, who was bilingual and had met Borges in 1928, translated *Fictions* in 1951 with Paul Verdevoye. Borges later said 'Ibarra knows me more intimately than anybody else.'[21] Caillois himself translated *El Aleph* in 1953 with a title Borges never used, *Labyrinthes*. So from 1953 Borges's best work, his mind-teasers, were available in French. The German and English translations of Borges would also adopt Caillois's title *Labyrinths* in 1961. Caillois, an astute intellectual, co-founder with Georges Bataille of the College of Sociology, and a fringe member of Breton's late 1930s Surrealist group, was the promoter of Borges in Europe. He was responsible for making Borges far more cosmopolitan than

he really was, excising Argentine texts like 'The South'. Borges told
Alberto Manguel: 'I'm an invention of Caillois',[22] and this was literally
true as Caillois bleached out Borges's Argentineness. When Borges
won the 1961 Prix Formentor with Samuel Beckett, which confirmed
his cult status, Caillois was on the jury. Caillois knew Borges
personally, found him original, a vertiginous reasoner, but glacially
unattached. Borges and Caillois came to blows publicly in 1941
and 1942 in the pages of *Sur* over the history of the detective story,
which Borges insisted originated with Poe and not a minor French
writer called Fosca; Caillois was 'not wrong, just inept'. Borges
never dedicated anything to Caillois, or included him as a friend
inside his fictions.[23]

The 1940s saw Borges become the secret mentor or antagonist
to the following generation. With hindsight, it's easy to discern a
pre-Borges attitude to writing and a post-Borges one. Julio Cortázar
(1914–1984) is a good example. Although he had published sonnets
and critical articles under a pseudonym Julio Denis, it was Borges
who launched him as the short story rival to himself by publishing
his 'Casa tomada' in the library magazine Borges edited, *Los Anales
de Buenos Aires*, in 1946. It was illustrated with two pencil drawings
by Norah Borges. In the same number Borges published his
Minotaur subversion 'The House of Asterion'. Years later, Cortázar
would say that what Borges taught him was 'rigour', both economy
of style and condensed thinking. Much of Cortázar's work can be
seen as avoiding Borges, like writing novels or his fascination with
jazz, boxing, Surrealism, Jarry, Artaud and later, revolutionary
politics.

The same applies to Ernesto Sábato (b. 1911), who first met
Borges through Adolfo Bioy Casares in 1940. He defined his
rambling novels against Borges's concision. Sábato had given up
a promising career as a research physicist in Paris in order to explore
his own and society's anguishes and inner hells through fiction. He
remained a popularizer of the clash between the order of science and

Borges and Ernesto Sábato in a bar in Buenos Aires in the 1980s.

existentialism in all its forms, often writing for *Sur*. He had found his true vocation through a close friendship with the Canarian Surrealist Oscar Domínguez in Paris (they even hatched a suicide pact, which only Domínguez kept). In 1964 he defended Borges against the literal-minded nationalists of the right and left, and argued that Borges was radically Argentine in articulating the transitoriness of life in the vast city and expressing nostalgia, from his class perspective, for the outskirts, the tough gaucho and *guapo* way of life. However, he found him too bookish, anaemic and Byzantine, lacking in life, in generosity and sensibility to deal with the fate of Argentina. He fiddles with style, plays frivolously with ideas. Sábato rescued the humble poet in Borges for posterity, not the creator of the hyper-intellectualized fictions. If we invert Sábato's insights, we unearth his own messy, Dostoevskean novels. In *Abaddón el exterminador* (1974), Borges appears as a character, and in *Sobre héroes y tumbas* (1966), the blind form a sinister underground cult. Sábato appears as himself in a footnote to Borges's story 'The Immortal'. Later, a dialogue between Borges and Sábato was published. In old age, Sábato would also lose his sight. Sábato was the earliest critic to suggest a dual Borges: the poet he approved of, tied to Buenos Aires and the writer of Byzantine games who was cerebral, cool and anti-human. It set off a critical trend within Argentina that labelled Borges as not really Argentine, as too bookish and erudite, too cosmopolitan, a frigid, apolitical European in exile.

During the war, and under Peronism, Borges suffered what has become his most publicized love affair, with the writer and communist Estela Canto. In 1989 Canto wrote her version of this affair with a timid man, eighteen years her senior. He proposed marriage to her on a cement bench on the river coast between Adrogué and Mármol. She was willing to become his mistress, even marry him if they went to bed together, but he insisted it had to be marriage first. As mentioned earlier, he was not impotent, but was panicked and shameful about sex. She urged him to see a therapist, Dr Miguel Kohan-Miller, about his stammering and fear of public speaking, and he dedicated his complex story 'The Aleph' to her. Their bookish and lustful relationship began in August 1944, meeting

Borges and Estela
Canto, 1945.

125

at the Bioy Casares's. They would walk across Buenos Aires, and the Parque Lezama became their favoured meeting-place. This once-grand private garden was where Buenos Aires was first claimed for Spain, and on it is the Museo Histórico Nacional, with the Russian orthodox church on one side. It stands on a high bank which the river once lapped, and looks down over La Boca, the slum of Genoese immigrants that Borges refused to visit. Throughout this two-year, off-and-on affair, Borges would phone his mother, excuse his lateness, his not coming home to eat, until he had to introduce Estela Canto to her. The two women loathed each other. I've already alluded to Canto's view that Borges was clearly excited by her, that he had been to bed with few women. She was never attracted to him as a man; she, as a bohemian, preferred adventurers and spies and was sexually experienced. She loved talking books, but found his conventional manners stifling. They only ever kissed: 'His awkward, brusque, always inappropriate kisses were accepted condescendingly.'[24] Her analysis of his character is acute. He was, she wrote, a cautious man, scared of arousing scandal, who knew that he was different. The key to his mind and work was allusion, insinuation. They argued over authors; she had no time for Conrad or Stevenson, and he dismissed Thomas Mann and Chekhov. Henry James was a bone of contention. In the 1960s Alberto Manguel met her and evoked her dyed red hair and intense myopic eyes.

A few anecdotes stand out. Borges and Canto were arrested in the Parque Lezama for unseemly behaviour (holding hands? arms around each other? kissing?) and not having their ID cards with them. Borges managed to win the officer over and they were let off with a warning. He would often sing tangos at the top of his voice. Borges also bought her what he called the Aleph, a child's kaleidoscope. Borges was working on his story 'The Aleph' at the time and dedicated it to Estela Canto who typed it up. Later, he gave her the manuscript and she sold it at Sotheby's for US $27,760. It took a week to write, and Borges had fun. His family was away in Montevideo. He worked at the library, lunched with Haydée Lange, went to the cinema, but sensed that his everyday life was false, that only the story 'The Aleph' was true.[25] We can read Borges's affair with Estela Canto back into the story for he must have known what kinds of men she was sexually attracted to. And he couldn't win her over with his strange mind, or stories. Estela Canto was clearly Dante's Beatrice to Borges, the promise of love and bliss. Finally, the letters that Borges wrote her, printed in her impressionistic biography, are vivid of a Borges in love. In one undated letter from Adrogué, he admits he nearly cried when he passed Parque Lezama without her. If she would help him, he would overcome his obsessions (what did he mean by that?). In another postcard, in English, he mentions his 'bodily pang of being separated from you',[26] and swears that they'd be happy together and 'sometimes speechless and most gloriously silly'. 'The Aleph' is a 'desperate love letter to Estela' suggested José Emilio Pacheco; 'I'd been jilted by Beatriz Viterbo', said Borges.[27] Later in 1955, when blind and Director of the National Library, Estela Canto would turn up on the steps and hector Borges – 'You promised to marry me . . . ' – and insult him whenever she could. Whatever later biographers affirm, her insights into his mind, behaviour and writing strike me as spot on.

In 1946 Norah Lange and Oliverio Girondo finally married. If Norah Lange was indeed the love of Borges's life (which I doubt), this would have been the final nail in the coffin, although she had brushed him aside ages before. Did the affair with Estela Canto bury this earlier wound? I believe it did, but he wrote a strange story about not being able to forget called 'The Zahir', on the surface another tale about his insomnia, like 'Funes, His Memory', generated by his accident and fear of losing his mind. In this story he is 'Borges', and a woman called Teodelina Villar dies. She's a typical upper-classy *porteña* into fashion, Paris, Hollywood; she's conventional and *cursi* ('vulgar') and she became a model. Her fortunes change and she dies in poverty in the *barrio sur*. In a bar on the corner of Chile and Tacuarí streets (where in fact Estela Canto lived), Borges accepts a zahir coin as change from a beer and gets giddy, wanders the streets, strangely happy. Was he drunk? He decides to get rid of the coin, writes a fantastic story, but cannot forget it. The coin becomes an obsession, an *idée fixe*, he sees a specialist, is scared of going mad, like Julia, Teodelina's sister. Many learned references are woven into this tale about not being able to forget, where the passing of time makes things worse, and where everything, a whole life in all its details, can be implied from this one coin, even God. My guess is that it's Estela, not Norah, who he cannot forget. John Barth simply called it a 'love story'.

Under Perón, Borges collected his essays with the aggressive title *Otras inquisiciones* in 1952 ('Other Inquisitions', a sequel to his suppressed 1926 book *Inquisiciones*). This exciting book, with the fictions of *Ficciones* and *El Aleph*, is the third in the trinity of his great works. These wide ranging, teasing essays are completely original. They are not conventional book reviews, nor literary essays in the Virginia Woolf or Cyril Connolly mould. They all arise from reading, but comment on apparently random details. All were published in magazines first. They jump around from Kafka to Wells, W. H. Hudson, Pascal, Keats, Beckford, Coleridge, Quevedo, Wilde, Américo Castro in unpredictable, quirky ways (who on earth would group those authors?). This is a new genre between his fictions (equally bookish and cheekily learned) and the hoax reviews, that 'seudoerudition' (his noun) that Borges made his own. I repeat; he had no time for 'bibliographies', dates, histories; he was for hedonism, pleasure-reading. Robert Graves accused him of not being historical in his sources, so that you never knew if he invented a quotation or not (Borges would laugh at this, that was the point of his anti-bibliographic writing). In 1964 Sábato accused him of an 'irriguroso conocimiento' ('lack of rigour in his knowledge'), displaying a dilettante's 'disparatada mezcla' ('crazy mixture'),[28] missing the point that this is his freedom and strength. More recently, Juan José Sebreli contrasted Borges with Sartre and underlined the former's avoidance of history, psychology, sociology and sexuality. He defined Borges's erudition as 'extravagant and unilateral',[29] based on caprice and random reading, many encyclopaedias, much pastiche and plagiarism. That flicking-through-books that characterized his hedonistic reading method, what Borges himself called 'pure aesthetic pleasure';[30] he was Barthian before Barthes. Sebreli quotes Borges's close friend Néstor Ibarra: 'Borges erudite? I would even worry about calling him learned. What a chaos of reading.' But that's exactly the point. In the 1940s in Argentina, Borges's strangeness was based on this apparently random learning. When the exiled English writer Christopher Isherwood visited Buenos Aires in 1948 he called on Borges, and characterized him as an 'extraordinary scholar' (not poet or short story writer), who could quote entire passages from the 'most unexpected authors, with very amusing and subtle comments'.[31] Exactly. His essays had made Borges the talk of the town.

No doubt, then, about his local prestige. In 1947 the English poet and critic G. S. Fraser met Borges, already the most 'original living Argentine writer' and the 'last great master of the discursive English essay' (Fraser read him too literally). But he was perceptive about the man himself as 'rather dry, sad and morose'; 'his emotions are coiled and compressed' and noticed his 'touch of malice' (that Imp in him). Borges avoided 'obvious rhetoric' to reveal a 'rare combination of density with ease' (that is, learning and humour). He looked like a great 'teddy-bear' and had a 'quite exceptional integrity of mind'.[32]

6

From Blindness to Geneva

When Perón was ousted from the Casa Rosada by a military coup
in September 1955, Borges, like many of the middle class urban anti-
Peronists, took to the streets and became hoarse with shouting.
Perón took refuge in the Paraguayan embassy, boarded a warship
for Asunción, and finally ended up in exile in Franco's Madrid. In a
recent poll, Borges and Perón were recognized as Argentina's two
most famous men. Tomás Eloy Martínez sees this period as a duel
between the two, which Perón won. For Borges, though, this ridding
of a tyrant, 'a scoundrel' he once said, was tempered by his acceptance
that 1955 was the year of his final, fated blindness. Much of the darkness in his 1940s work was literal, for he struggled to read and write.
Thus blindness terminated his creative bout and his amazing fictions
and essays. That he could not read what he had just written was the
final straw. He would not write that way again, and desisted from
writing stories until 1970 with *El informe de Brodie*, and later *El libro de
arena* in 1975. These vastly different stories had to be dictated, and
remain loose and 'oral', what he called 'straightforward story-telling'.[1]
Five of the stories of *El informe de Brodie*, for example, call attention
to a 'he told me' or 'they say', somebody telling the narrator a story.
Borges had to sacrifice that stunning rigour, those odd adjectives and
taut syntax. As J. M. Coetzee noted, there's much tired writing in
them and they 'add nothing to his stature'.[2] Earlier, the critic Michael
Wood thought the same: Borges's later work was close to boredom,
much overrated.[3]

I've referred to some of these later stories already, though the most revealing is 'Guayaquil', famous in Latin American lore as the Ecuadorian city where the liberators Simón Bolívar and San Martín met alone in 1823 and talked for several hours. San Martín wanted to restore an Incan monarchy, then backed away, and died in exile in France. Nobody knows what they said to each other. Borges opens his story by affirming that he will never get to see the Higuerota peak, or the waters of the Golfo Plácido, with more references to Estado Occidente and Sulaco. Nothing in the story explains these obvious references to Joseph Conrad's *Nostromo* (1904), where Conrad, long Borges's favourite novelist because he mixes adventure and Quevedan *desengaño* (waking up to the truth), invented a Latin American republic torn apart by dictators and the thirst for gold (and wrote the first novel about Latin America). He'll never get there because it's fiction anyhow. A clue to Conrad in the story is his real Polish name, Korzeniovski, and the apocryphal history book that Conrad invented in his novel, Avellanos's *Historia de cincuenta años de desgobierno* (this fake erudition is Conrad's Borgesian touch). The patrician narrator, with Argentine history running through his veins, meets an exiled Jewish historian, who persuades the narrator that he should desist from going to inspect newfound letters from Bolívar in Avellanos's archive. So the narrator and Zimmermann relive the Bolívar and San Martín confrontation, and the narrator is reminded that Schopenhauer, on his bookshelf, didn't believe in history anyhow. Zimmermann says that the narrator probably never wanted to leave his house. Is Latin America more real in Conrad? Can you only know literature, not the real world? Yet, there's a sense of thankful defeat. The last sentence is in French: 'Mon siège est fait', a proverb derived from the Abbé Vertot suggesting that the charms of narrative outweigh strict historical truth, Borges's Schopenhauerian poetics. The title story 'Brodie's Report' is a faked anthropological and Swiftian journey into the land of the Yahoos. I can imagine Borges chuckling as he deals with the poets. They string enigmatic words together, then shout them from the centre of a circle formed by witch doctors. If the poet's words work, everybody moves away in silence 'under a holy dread'. Not even the poet's mother will speak to him. He's no longer a man, but a God and can be killed. He seeks refuge in the deserts of the north. This is not an allegory about divine powers, or a replay of Plato's banishment of the Dyonisiac poets, but a joke.

Another story, 'Ulrikke', dubbed by Edwin Williamson as the most directly autobiographical, if not confessional, of all his stories,[4] has the Colombian narrating professor meet Ulrikke in York. She's a tall, thin and mysterious Norwegian feminist. After a walk to Thorgate, he was already in love. She was leaving for London, to follow De Quincey's trails. He kisses her and she offers herself to him in the inn. Wolves howl (a joke allusion to the attacking Vikings). They nickname each other Sigurd and Brynhild, lovers in the Icelandic *Völsunga* saga, as if the sword in the bed between them is finally removed. He 'possessed' her image. This story's epigraph is engraved on Borges's Genevan tomb. Why the sword between them, now removed? Why De Quincey, who quested for the young whore Ann? Why could he only possess an 'image'? Borges refers to an ideal of the mind (others are always images in our minds). Like Dante with the long-dead Beatrice, you can only possess in the mind. Edwin Williamson sees this as Borges's final relinquishing of Norah Lange and accepting that María Kodama has replaced her, a late flowering of love and happiness, but a biographic explanation reduces the story. In the 1981 poem 'Nostalgia del presente' ('Nostalgia for the Present'), *dicha*, bliss in Spanish, is being next to her in the present moment, though 'she' isn't named. Borges did spend happy days in Iceland with María Kodama, but I would rather read 'Ulrikke' as a summation of an old blind man's ideal of love in the mind, where literature (Icelandic sagas, De Quincey) is deeply shared. In 1996 Susan Sontag invoked this bookish quality in Borges: 'We are still learning from you', especially an indebtedness to literature. If books disappear, human beings will too. Books are much more than escapism, she wrote, 'they are a way of being fully human'.[5] His old friend Adolfo Bioy Casares once complained that Borges put books before truth.[6] What I would add, concerning Borges, is that sharing a passion for the same books is the ultimate erotic ideal, reading together, a Paolo and Francesca syndrome.

Nevertheless, in terms of value and the canon, had Borges only written his post-1950s work of oral tales and modest, bare poems, he would have returned to being a Pierre Menard, a footnote in literary histories. This period, dominated by blindness, also, paradoxically, led to his fame, beyond the earlier cult readership, recognized everywhere he went and imitated by Argentines for his distinct voice, if he was ever actually read by so many admirers. Blindness and fame arrived together.

At first, Borges's 1955 blindness forced him to write poems. He had to abandon free verse as he needed mnemonic devices like metre, rhyme and assonance to remember what he was dictating or composing in his mind. Luckily, Borges still possessed a fabulous memory. 'I had to fall back on memory', he wrote,[7] for he knew why he had been training his memory for decades. He also noted that many of his post-1955 poems had some narrative thread, to guide him. His 'Poema de los dones' ('Poem of the Gifts'), dedicated to María Esther Vázquez , his crush in the 1960s and later biographer (though he dropped this dedication after she refused to marry him), clarifies his life's irony that God 'me dio a la vez los libros y la noche' ('gave me books and the night at the same time')[8] for he was nominated by Victoria Ocampo and others as a possible Director of the Biblioteca Nacional on calle México 564 (the building was originally built for the National Lottery in 1901). He was appointed and thus reinstated as a librarian, right at the top, in the year of his definitive blindness. A further oddity is that the National Library

Borges at his desk in the National Library.

had been run twice before by blind men, first the writer José
Mármol, from 1858 to 1871 (author of *Amalia*, a vast realist novel
about Rosas's dictatorship) and then Borges's admired Paul
Groussac from 1885 to 1929. Groussac (1848–1929) was another
surprising mentor, a French intellectual who had emigrated to
Buenos Aires, taught Borges to be 'intelligent and just' and alerted
him against the innate baroque convolutions of the Spanish tradition.
Borges sat next to the round desk that Groussac had had specially
built, with Piranesi prints on the wall, and revolving bookcases with
his favourite reference works. Behind his mahogany table he would
remain as nominal director for eighteen years, until 1973, when he
was aided by José Edmundo Clemente who was already co-editing
books with him and who, in reality, ran the library. The *Paris
Review* interviewer cited a secretary who took down his letters and
poems confirming that there were always jokes, little 'practical
jokes'.[9] In this library, he was surrounded by 900,000 books that
he couldn't read, a blind library. Borges tapped his way round with
his cane, he who'd thought that Paradise 'came in the form of a

134

library'.[10] In the introduction to *El hacedor* (1960), dedicated to
Leopoldo Lugones, Borges wrote that the noises of the plaza stayed
behind as 'I enter the Library' and evoked how he physically felt
the 'gravitation of the books, their serene order and dried time and
conserved so magically in the pages'. It's odd, but Borges always
pointed to the materiality of books, exact editions, their feel and
smell and the physicality of aesthetics. 'Beauty', he said in 1977
'is a physical sensation, something we feel in our bodies'.[11] His
alter-ego Juan Dahlmann of 'The South' nearly died in his rush
to fondle an edition of *The Arabian Nights*.

In 1960 Borges was persuaded by his publisher to empty his draw-
ers. He collected bits and pieces that he'd written more for the joy
of writing than thinking of publishing and had the prose and poetry
medley titled *El hacedor* ('The Maker or Poet'). The first English
translation foolishly adopted the title, already in English, of the
second text, *Dreamtigers*, and made the collection more exotic
sounding (Andrew Hurley restored it to *The Maker*). The opening
piece dramatizes the arrival of blindness in Homer. The first
Homer was alive, like Borges himself, in the world of the senses,
but gradually the beautiful universe started to abandon him. When
he knew he was going blind, he screamed aloud, for stoicism had
not been invented. Then he calmed down and turned to memory
'which seemed interminable', like Funes in his dark room, and
thereby rescued lost memories. He remembered the weight of a
bronze dagger and then a woman. He could still challenge love
and take risks, dream and write. Borges did not commit suicide
with the onset of blindness, but became a different writer, a minor
but moving poet. In this miscellany, Borges included his parable,
'Borges and I'.

   In *El oro de los tigres* ('The Gold of the Tigers') of 1972 Borges
returned to his destiny as 'El ciego' ('The Blindman'). He has been
stripped of the diverse world, of faces, of books and left with

memory, a kind of forgetting. He's in the dark, alone, 'shaping his insipid universe'.[12] All his life 'el tiempo minucioso' ('meticulous time') has been stealing the visible world, even the mirrors he detested are grey. He can only smell a rose in the shadows, see yellow forms and inner nightmares. But this self-pity is only part of the story; the other is love, as we'll see.

Another new start for the now blind Borges was learning and teaching of Anglo-Saxon, then Old Norse and Icelandic, with a group of adoring students that would include María Kodama. He had always been struck by Norse literatures; in 1933 he'd published *Las kennigar*, a short study of 'kenniger' or stock metaphor. He and his women students met on Saturdays in cafés like the Richmond on calle Florida, and it became a passion, derived, he felt, from his Northumbrian grandmother. In a lecture on blindness in 1977, Borges suggested that blindness let him grasp that poetry was first music (sounds), that learning Anglo-Saxon confirmed that each word in a foreign language is music, a poem in itself. Blindness redefined his literary canon with Homer and then Milton, Prescott, Groussac and Joyce, who learnt Norwegian in order to write to Ibsen.

From 1961 and the sharing of the publishers' Prix Formentor with Samuel Beckett (six international publishers had put up the money and promised publication and translations), Borges, who was already 62, began travelling. He obviously needed a helper. First it was with his mother and then, when she became too old, with María Esther Vázquez and to his death with María Kodama (occasionally some others like Norman Thomas di Giovanni). Over these years of his fame, he received countless honorary degrees (Oxford, Harvard, Sorbonne, Cambridge) and further prizes (Cervantes, Jerusalem, T. S. Eliot, etc.). About that Formentor Prize (named after a hotel in Mallorca), he wrote: 'As a consequence of that prize, my books mushroomed overnight throughout the western world.'[13] Just looking at the dates of his translations into English or

German (all post-1961, apart from the French), confirms this sudden, late notoriety. Because he attained fame abroad, he became a public figure at home (a snobbish Argentine trait), but he was already in his sixties.

Borges's writings depended on help; he had to dictate and revise when the dictation was read aloud back to him. It lead to immense activity over the years, at first with his mother, then a string of women friends and crushes like Betina Edelberg, Margarita Guerrero and the already mentioned Alicia Jurado, María Kodama and María Esther Vázquez. In 1979 he published most of these collaborations in one volume of 989 pages. It includes nearly all his work with Adolfo Bioy Casares and studies on Lugones, on *Martín Fierro*, on Buddhism, as well as anthologies on Anglo Saxon, English and medieval German literature, and a quirky book of Imaginary Beings.

During these blind years, Borges continued to live on calle Maipú 994 with his mother until she arranged his church marriage in 1967 to Elsa Astete Millán, an early flame from the 1930s recently widowed. They moved to a flat near the National Library on avenida Belgrano 1377, 8A. But the three-year marriage was a disaster. Borges remained mummy's boy, missed his narrow iron bed and his freedom. He complained that his wife never dreamed, didn't talk books. His American translator Norman Thomas di Giovanni, then living in Buenos Aires and translating with Borges every afternoon, helped him break free of this marriage. Borges told his wife that he'd be back after a trip to Córdoba, but sent his lawyer round and moved back to his real home. His wife accused him publicly of being a coward, not facing her with his desire for a separation.

Borges continued to work at the National Library until he resigned in 1973, faced with the absurd return of Perón to a euphoric Argentina trying to redefine itself as left-wing Peronist, sparked off by guerrilla movements and the Cuban revolution. It was around these politicized 1970s that the hostile view of Borges as a conservative took precedence in the public eye, disguising the mischievous *enfant terrible* that he was. He had no time for the revolutionaries, for Che Guevara and for mobs, and celebrated when the military coup ended Perón's widow's grotesque government in 1976. He would be haunted by a lunch with the generals who he likened to gentlemen. Because he didn't read the papers or listen to the radio he had no inkling that they aired their love for their country while disappearing thousands of young people, without trial, in truly sadistic ways, so that Argentina became tainted with the term 'desaparecidos' (as many as 30,000 of them). When he was taken to one of the later trials in 1985 and heard what had actually gone on, he was appalled and had to leave the courtroom nauseated. Earlier, he had publicly approved of President Johnson's invasion of Santo Domingo in 1965. He famously also had a meal with General Pinochet in Chile during his visit to receive an honorary doctorate from the Catholic university of Santiago (not a medal from the tyrant as rumour had it then). Indeed, rumours flourish about his reactionary attitudes. Recently, a newspaper asserted that Borges and Bioy Casares had sent a telegram congratulating the Mexican president Gustavo Díaz Ordaz on massacring some 300 student demonstrators in 1968 in Tlatelolco. These acts of political naïvety tarred the image of Borges for generations of left-thinking readers and intellectuals who confused the old man with the adventurous Borges, before blindness.

I met him twice in 1976

However, 1975 was also the year his mother died, aged 99. His grief was terrible, but he continued to live on in his room on calle Maipú, leaving his mother's room untouched, a museum. Harold Bloom refers to 'an astonishing closeness' between mother and son and certainly it was the defining relationship of his life. A few days after her death he published one of his best known poems, lamenting her death, a sonnet titled 'El remordimiento' ('Remorse'), collected in *La moneda de hierro* (1976), illustrated by Antonio Berni, announcing that he had 'committed the worst of sins a man can

Borges and his mother, Leonor Acevedo, in London in 1963.

commit', not having been happy. His parents had gifted him life, but he had defrauded them and his art had simply 'woven nothing-nesses' ('entreteje naderías'), for he hadn't been brave, just a 'des-dichado' (like in Nerval's sonnet). This poem stands for much that he wrote over his last years, returning to poetry that was sincere, direct and traditional, a prosaic reflection of his readings, his travels and his ups and downs in love. It is ironic that Borges, the grand ironist, felt that poetry dealt with emotional truth, the elemen-tary feelings that all people share. And poems could be written in his mind, and then dictated. However, he did find a late ripeness and *dicha* (happiness) in his relationship with María Kodama and his studying of the old Nordic texts. Most of his life he had been unhappy in love. His key story 'The Aleph' traces his adoration of a silly woman, Beatriz Viterbo (who he also glimpses in his mystical vision through the Aleph), only saved by oblivion by slowly deleting her image after her death (time cures lovesickness). In a commen-tary on Dante's *Commedia* about Dante and Beatrice (the name of the woman who jilted 'Borges' in 'The Aleph'), Borges thinks of the adulterous lovers Paolo and Francesca 'united forever in their Hell. With terrible love, with anxiety, with admiration, with envy.'[14] That last word 'envy' is Borges's confession that he had never given himself up to sexual passion. Alberto Manguel met Borges while he worked in the Anglo-German bookshop Pygmalion in 1965 and often went to read for him after hours, or took him to the cinema. He characterized Borges as a fumbling dream-lover, with his ancient mother as companion and Beppo, a large white Angoran cat named after Byron's narrative poem, the most famous in Argentine literature according to Alan Pauls.[15]

A critique of Borges's place in Argentina issued from the novelist V. S. Naipaul (b. 1932), who visited Buenos Aires in 1972 with his mistress to explore the enigma of the country for the *New York Review of Books*. Naipaul considered Borges's prestige as inflated and bogus. He saw him rather as a 'sweet and melancholic poet', a writer of direct prose (he evidently hadn't yet read the 1940s work). He heard him talk about Old English, Chesterton, Kipling in a courteous way. The old man was carefully dressed, self-effacing, protecting his privacy. Naipaul summed up: 'a curiously colonial performance', as if he stood for the enigma of Argentina, and decided that 'Borges has not hallowed Buenos Aires', again probably unaware how identified with his city Borges had been before, though not in novels like Dickens or Galdós or Balzac.[16] Another poet witness to Borges's always pertinent literary chatter was Willis Barnstone, who found him childlike, full of humour, and always enjoying things, to the point, contradicting Naipaul, that 'Borges was the centre of the Argentine experience'.[17]

Another celebrated witticism and poem came from the Falklands/Malvinas war in 1982 when the generals running the country mistakenly invaded some unwanted British colonies, instead of waiting and receiving them. Argentina's reward was nearly 1,000 pointless deaths. Borges, anglophile, stated in an interview that infuriated fellow Argentines that the war was like two bald men fighting over a comb. In his anti-war sonnet of 1982 two men who could have been friends, Juan López and Juan Ward, met on the island 'and each one of the two was Cain, and each one Abel'. They were buried together. Snow and corruption know them.[18] The 'poem', repeated and cited, became an anti-war ditty. Borges told Alberto Manguel that Mrs Thatcher and Galtieri were one and the same person.[19] The poem ended by alluding to a crazy historical moment that nobody could understand.

A crucial figure in lifting Borges out of his gloom and sense of defeat since his blindness was the American-born translator Norman Thomas di Giovanni (b. 1933), one of the most acute witnesses to Borges's later creativity, who provoked Borges to start writing again, dictating stories, poems and his memoirs. They met at Harvard in 1967 when Borges was giving the Charles Eliot Norton lectures. Di Giovanni had just published a bilingual anthology of the poet-scholar Jorge Guillén's work and offered to do the same for Borges, who jumped at the idea; he'd always seen himself as foremost a poet. Di Giovanni moved to Buenos Aires in November 1968 and remained for three and a half years, working most week-days with Borges at the Biblioteca Nacional. He'd arranged for *The New Yorker* to take whatever they translated and took a percentage to survive in Buenos Aires. He persuaded Borges to write his memoirs in English (there is no Spanish original; later Spanish translations are by others). Di Giovanni was hard working and a teaser. These joint translations or versions remain vivid. He also brought Borges to London in 1967, a visit that confirmed Borges's status as a literary grandmaster. But he too suffered from one of Borges's sudden changes of moods, a peevish streak, and between one course and another in Bioy Casares's dining room had his co-translating terminated. Since then, Borges's widow commissioned a new set of translations into English that would not depend on

Borges having collaborated, with Andrew Hurley translating the fictions.[20]

Borges's companion over the last decade of his life, though they never actually lived together in Buenos Aires, was María Kodama (b. 1937), a half-Japanese ex-student. While they were both in Geneva, where she had taken him in November 1985, sick with liver cancer, they were married by proxy in Paraguay in April 1986 (there was no divorce in Argentina at the time). He died on 14 June 1986 at his rented home and is buried in the Plainpalais cemetery (G-735), near Jean Calvin's grave. Ten years of posthumous legal wrangles followed; for example, his sister Norah and her two sons Miguel and Luis sued for the repatriation of Borges's remains from Geneva, grounded on a nullified marriage to María Kodama, but failed.[21] The tombstone in Geneva, sculpted by Eduardo Longato, has on one side the epigraph from his story 'Ulrikke' from *The Book of Sand*. It's a quotation from the Volsunga Saga: *Hann tekr sverthit Gram ok leggr i methal thiera bert*. Translated it means 'He took his sword, Gram, and placed the naked metal between the two.' This

Borges and María Kodama in Paris in 1986.

Nordic echo was close to Borges's heart as in reading and teaching Anglo Saxon and Icelandic he at last felt at ease, surrounded by admiring students, never alone. He'd also first read this saga as a boy in William Morris's translation. On the reverse side of the tomb is an engraved shield from the Sutton Hoo treasure with a quotation from the 'Battle of Maldon', written *c.* AD 1000 and translated by Borges and María Kodama as 'be not afraid'. The tombstone is in effect a lapidary anthology of how Borges saw himself at the end of his life with María Kodama.

In these last years Borges broke relations with his intimate friend Adolfo Bioy Casares and with his close sister Norah (though they made it up just before he died) and her two sons Luis and Miguel, with whom he never spoke again (there had been confusion over an account, and financial recriminations). He changed his 1970 will, which was in their favour, and left all to María Kodama. He also decided to be buried, rather than cremated, in Geneva, and not lie in the grand Recoleta cemetery in Buenos Aires, about which he had penned early poems (where his mother lies; his father was buried in the Cementerio Británico). Did Borges choose to return to the city of his adolescence because he was at last happy in his relationship with María Kodama? Did he really want to die in peace and anonymously, far from from prying journalists? Was it just another of his *enfant terrible* whims? Borges wrote a press release, read by his lawyer in Buenos Aires, confirming that 'María Kodama is the most irreproachable person, ethically and morally, that I have known in my entire life. With her I have finally found happiness.'[22] There is some truth that what Borges learnt from María Kodama's feminism (evident in the story 'Ulrikke') had to do with independence. Kodama now directs a Borges foundation and continues to publish his work, from books he himself had banned to compilations of his journalism and uncollected bits and pieces. She has taken several critics to court or has been taken herself, including a case against Borges's faithful maid

see biblio

~~ Epifanía Uveda de Robledo (known as Fanny), who was kicked out
of the tiny Maipú flat and left in the street. She now lives in La
Boca, and survives thanks to some of Borges's friends. So the last
and posthumous years have been bitter. There are rival Borges
centres like Jorge Helft's Fundación San Telmo or Antonio Carrizo's
✗ collection. All this is gossip and doesn't enter the work.

So from blindness in 1955 to death in 1986, we have two books
of oral stories that are minor works, several collections of quiet,
honest poems, countless prologues, but not one of his strange critical
essays, as he had ceased reading new work. A writer taken as daring and strange in the 1960s had not kept up with current writing,
and in fact, had developed a quirky canon of what he considered
the best literature that got weirder the closer the writers came to
being his contemporaries. His inability to appreciate French literature, especially Proust and Flaubert (he admitted never having read
Balzac), or Surrealism or music and most realist fiction or Lorca or
Rilke, form part of his literary persona and generate the baffling
allusions and clues in his work. For Borges the supreme novelist
was Conrad. In adventure novels, he said, what counts are the
adventures not the characters. He could talk endlessly of Coleridge
as if he still lived and claimed that Robert Louis Stevenson was
his best friend.

As a writer Borges was uninterested in creating memorable characters (most of his stories hinge on embodied ideas). He said that
'I've never created a character. It's always me, subtly disguised.'[23]
As a quasi-solipsist, perhaps, he just couldn't perceive the quiddity
of other people. Just as his characters suddenly change into their
opposite, so Borges could cut people out of his life. He also severed
his own past selves (especially the *ultraísta* and the fake patriot or
criollo), and constantly revised his texts and books, excising,
adding, fiddling. He once joked that misprints improved his work.
You sense that he always projected his love on to women and didn't

really listen to what other people had to say (his interviews are repetitive). María Esther Vázquez, who should know, claimed that he fell in love every three or four years. He acted as a kind of Shavian Pygmalion, a Professor Higgins (according to Rodríguez Monegal) to his devoted women admirers and students. Despite the presence of María Kodama, Borges fell, for example, for a young woman Viviana Aguilar, dedicated a poem 'Al olvidar un sueño' ('On Forgetting a Dream') in *La cifra* (1981), to her. She worked in the bookshop La Ciudad in the smart Galería del Este that linked calle Maipú with Florida, just across from where Borges lived, where he went every day. It could be claimed that Borges became famous abroad, through translation, just because nothing was known about him and readers could just read him, amazed, out of context, creating their own image of a blind guru. His stories and parables of the 1940s (*Ficciones*, *El Aleph*) remain by far the best work and alone justify his reputation (he has become an adjective, 'Borgesian'). Biographies, meanwhile, will scan the enigmatic man and not respect his privacy that he justified as solipsism, his gentlemanly reticence about his sexuality (did he go to bed with women, was he a masturbator, where did his sexual drive take him?). I feel the clues to his rich imagination lie with his parents: the cultural and sexual split between them, the *criollo* versus the English, becoming his own inner bickering, the two Borgeses of his parable. His literary personality remains locked up in his stories and in his reader's notes. However, Alicia Jurado warns those of us who didn't get close to the man as she did from 1954 until his death that 'in his work you'll find only a part of his complex personality; the rest, all that I knew and loved, is lost forever'; her version of the dictum that when an old man dies a library is lost.

His influence has been enormous. Countless Borges tales, that are in fact parodies, have been written, epitomized in Bruce Chatwin's 'The Estate of Maximilian Tod', and by writers as diverse as José Emilio Pacheco, Ray Bradbury, José Balza, Umberto Eco,

Juan José Arreola, Augusto Monterroso, Enrique Vila-Matas, Italo Calvino, Peter Carey, Ignacio Padilla and Zadie Smith, many who did not stick to Borges's precision, his brevity. He appears in Donald Cammell and Nicolas Roeg's film *Performance* (1970), as modish as Mick Jagger himself in the film, a re-working of the best story, 'The South'. Bertolucci filmed the story 'Theme of the Traitor and the Hero' in 1969–70 as 'The Spider's Stratagem'; he is alluded to by Jean-Luc Godard. Borges would say that his stories have been written by literature itself, the author simply irrelevant. His legacy is that inversion of the writer/reader pact. It's the reader who writes the books that fill the library. No wonder Borges wrote so little that he thought would last, for too much has already been written. In 1964, in the prologue to his poems *El otro, el mismo*, he summarized his own life: 'Curious fate that of a writer. At first he's baroque, vainly baroque, and after years he manages to attain, if the stars are favourable, not simplicity, which is nothing, but a secret and modest complexity.'[24] That secret lies buried in the poems, not in some biographic fiction, and only reading them as a kind of magic will reveal anything. Borges told Bernard Pivot on his TV show in Paris in 1980 that all his stories had a source in personal experience never revealed to the reader – 'nobody has the right to confess secrets' – but he did tell them as allegory. Borges closes his inventive and erudite 'Nueva refutación del tiempo' ('A New Refutation of Time'), an idealist fantasy published privately in 1946, with his realisation that you cannot deny time passing or the self. Man's destiny is terrifying because it's 'irreversible and made of iron'.[25] He confesses that time is his substance; time is a river that carries him off, but he is the river, to end: 'El mundo, desgraciadamente, es real; yo, desgraciadamente, soy Borges' ('The world, unfortunately, is real; I, unfortunately, am Borges'). Here's the crux of his life, what Enrique Pezzoni, the last editor of *Sur*, called the most intensely autobiographic moment in Borges's work, a *cri de coeur*.[26] Literature, reading, the imagination cannot save anybody,

Borges, probably taken in the National Library.

no 'secret miracle'. Borges died reciting Verlaine, a poet read and learnt by heart as a boy poet in Geneva, and who in 'Otro poema de los dones' ('Another Poem of the Gifts') is 'innocent as a bird'.[27] Borges once boasted 'Creo no tener un solo enemigo' ('I do not believe that I have one single enemy'),[28] and that self-assessment stands for one facet of the gentle, teasing man he was. Ibarra agreed that Borges was 'the best-humoured man I ever met'.[29] Paul Theroux captured this quality in his typical thorough way. Borges was close to being 'angelic', yet had something of the charlatan in him. He laughed hard at his own jokes, revealing yellow teeth, and listened attentively. He was both sage and clown, but never the fool. He had met and read to Borges in his Maipú flat in 1972, calling him the gentlest of men. Not an ounce of violence in his breathless, staccato way of talking, or in his gestures.[30] However, Jean-Pierre Bernès was at his death bed and called Borges 'before all else a poet, always rebelling against everything, but peaceful'.

The editor of his French editions

That last insight about 'rebelling' brings Borges close to Herbert Read's 'gentle anarchist' and his own father's preference for the anarchism of Spencer over Bakunin. This last insight approaches that irreverence I noted at the start as the core of his personality, that disparity between the person and his work remarked on by Victoria Ocampo.

Borges told Willis Barnstone that he thought of himself as not being a modern writer; in fact, he saw himself as a nineteenth-century writer, alienated from movements like Surrealism.[31] That was his paradox, for he also absorbed Joyce and strands of the avant-garde (Expressionist poetry, *ultraísmo*). His advice to his readers emerged from this eccentric modernity: read little but reread much; there is no difference between fact and fiction and all the past is but our memory of it. The late Uruguayan critic and Yale professor Emir Rodríguez Monegal wrote his biography to correct the view that Borges was that old Sage beloved of American students; rather he was 'terribly alone' (in 1978), a sad, old-fashioned, shy, very Argentine old gentleman.[32] It's this Argentine self that translation and fame have disguised.

References

Introduction

1 'Jorge Luis Borges', *The Times* (10 June 1986).
2 Carlos Fuentes, 'The Accidents of Time', in Norman Thomas di Giovanni, ed., *The Borges Tradition* (London, 1995), p. 53.
3 *La Nación* (21 September 2003), p. 2.
4 Rodrigo Fresán, *Página*, 12 (18 January 2005), www.pagina12web.com.ar/suplementos/radar.
5 Jorge Luis Borges, *Obras completas* (Buenos Aires, 1974), p. 808.
6 *Borges en Sur, 1931–1999* (Buenos Aires, 1999), p. 200.
7 Jorge Luis Borges, *Collected Fictions*, trans. Andrew Hurley (London, 1998), p. 207.
8 *Borges en Sur*, p. 244.
9 *Obras completas*, p. 911.
10 *Collected Fictions*, p. 327.
11 Pierre Boncenne, 'Jorge Luis Borges s'explique', *Magazine Lire* (September 1980), p. 34.
12 *Obras completas*, p. 854.
13 Ibid., p. 1115.
14 Ibid., pp. 1143–5.
15 Jorge Luis Borges, *Nueve ensayos dantescos*, intro. Marcos Ricardo Barnatán (Madrid, 1982), p. 150.
16 César Fernández Moreno, 'Weary of Labyrinths: An Interview with Jorge Luis Borges', *Encounter* (April 1969), pp. 3–14.
17 *Obras completas*, p. 273.
18 Georges Charbonnier, *Entretiens avec Jorge Luis Borges* (Paris, 1967), p. 20.
19 Norman Thomas di Giovanni, *The Lesson of the Master: On Borges and*

his Work (London, 2003), p. 47.

20 Fernando Sorrentino, *Siete conversaciones con Jorge Luis Borges* [1972] (Buenos Aires, 2001), p. 152.

21 Jorge Luis Borges, *Obras completas en colaboración* (Buenos Aires, 1979), p. 719.

22 *Obras completas*, p. 580.

23 *Borges en Sur*, p. 248.

24 Borges's title 'Historia del rey y de la cautiva' refers to nomadic Indians kidnapping European women, 'cautivas', rather than to a fairy tale.

25 *Collected Fictions*, p. 118.

26 Ibid., p. 220.

27 *Obras completas en colaboración*, pp. 728, 752.

28 Ibid., p. 774.

29 Ibid., p. 747.

30 *Collected Fictions*, p. 100.

31 Cristina Castello, 'Entrevista con María Kodama', *Cuadernos Hispanoamericanos*, 651–2 (Sep/Oct 2004), pp. 219–30.

32 Emir Rodríguez Monegal, 'Borges: el lector como escritor', *Convergencias/divergencias/incidencias* (Barcelona, 1973), pp. 290–4.

33 *Collected Fictions*, p. 191.

34 Jorge Luis Borges, *Oeuvres complètes*, 1, ed. Jean Pierre Bernès (Paris, 1993), p. 1248.

35 Epifanía Uveda de Robledo and Alejandro Vaccaro, *El señor Borges* (Buenos Aires, 2004), p. 142.

36 Ibid., p. 144.

1 Buenos Aires to Palermo

1 Jorge Luis Borges, *Collected Fictions*, trans. Andrew Hurley (London, 1998), p. 131.

2 Willis Barnstone, *Borges at Eighty: Conversations* (Bloomington, IN, 1982), p. 34.

3 Jorge Luis Borges, *The Aleph and Other Stories, 1933–1969*, Norman Thomas di Giovanni, trans. and ed. in collaboration with the author (New York, 1970), p. 211.

4 Jorge Luis Borges, *Obras completas* (Buenos Aires, 1974), p. 51.

5 Ibid., pp. 86–7.
6 Ibid., pp. 828–9.
7 Estela Canto, *Borges a contraluz* (Madrid, 1989), p. 17.
8 Emir Rodríguez Monegal, *Jorge Luis Borges: A Literary Biography* (New York, 1978), p. 468.
9 Epifanía Uveda de Robledo and Alejandro Vaccaro, *El señor Borges* (Buenos Aires, 2004), p. 57.
10 *Obras completas*, p. 1,009.
11 *The Aleph*, p. 277.
12 Note Andrew Hurley's translation: 'That slightly wilful but never ostentatious "Argentinization"', *Collected Fictions*, p. 174.
13 *Obras completas*, p. 9.
14 Canto, *Borges a contraluz*, p. 49.
15 *Obras completas*, pp. 84–5.
16 *The Aleph*, p. 209.
17 *Obras completas*, p. 115.
18 *Borges en Sur, 1931–1980* (Buenos Aires, 1999), p. 73.
19 *Obras completas*, p. 117.
20 Ibid., p. 83.
21 Jorge Luis Borges and Ernesto Sábato, *Diálogos* (Buenos Aires, 1976), p. 161.
22 *Obras completas*, p. 870.
23 *Collected Fictions*, p. 294.
24 *Obras completas*, p. 1112.
25 Rubén Darío's poem 'Estío' from *Azul*, 1888.
26 *Obras completas*, pp. 824–5.
27 Ibid., p. 158.
28 Ibid., p. 793.
29 Ibid., pp. 1044–7.

2 Geneva and Spain

1 Jorge Luis Borges, *Atlas*, ed. and trans. María Kodama and Anthony Kerrigan (New York, 1986), p. 46.
2 Jorge Luis Borges, *Textos recobrados 1919–1929* (Buenos Aires, 1997), p. 220.
3 Jorge Luis Borges, *Obras completas* (Buenos Aires, 1974), p. 208.

4 Ibid., p. 250.

5 Jorge Luis Borges, *Prólogos* (Buenos Aires, 1975), p. 172.

6 *Obras completas*, p. 912.

7 *Textos recobrados*, p. 188.

8 Estela Canto, *Borges a contraluz* (Madrid, 1989), pp. 114–21.

9 Ibid., p. 98.

10 Jorge Luis Borges, *Collected Fictions*, trans. Andrew Hurley (London, 1998), p. 217.

11 Jorge Luis Borges, *Oeuvres complètes*, 1, ed. Jean Pierre Bernès (Paris, 1993), p. 1595.

12 Jorge Luis Borges, *Cartas del fervor: Correspondencia con Maurice Abramowicz y Jacobo Sureda 1919–1928* (Barcelona, 1999), p. 146.

13 Jean Pierre Bernès, *Album Jorge Luis Borges* (Paris, 1999), p. 82.

14 *Textos recobrados*, p. 112.

15 *Obras completas*, p. 852.

16 *Collected Fictions*, p. 432.

17 *Obras completas*, p. 1107.

18 Jorge Luis Borges, *The Aleph and Other Stories, 1933–1969*, Norman Thomas di Giovanni, trans. and ed. in collaboration with the author (New York, 1970), p. 218.

19 *Cartas del fervor*, p. 208. (note 12)

20 Carlos García, ed., *Macedonio Fernández/Jorge Luis Borges: Correspondencia 1922–1939. Crónica de una amistad* (Buenos Aires, 2000), p. 93.

21 *Obras completas*, p. 618.

22 *Macedonio Fernández/Jorge Luis Borges: Correspondencia*, pp. 62–3.

23 Ramón Gómez de la Serna, 'Norah Borges', *La Gaceta*, 346 (October 1999), pp. 39–44.

24 *The Aleph*, p. 221.

25 Ibid., p. 222.

26 Ibid., p. 222.

27 Jorge Luis Borges, *Inquisiciones* (Buenos Aires, 1993), p. 21.

28 *Obras completas*, p. 913.

29 María Esther Vázquez, *Borges: Esplendor y derrota* (Barcelona, 1996), p. 60.

30 Jorge Luis Borges, *Norah* (Milan, 1977), p. 9.

31 Sergio Baur, 'Norah Borges, musa de las vanguardias', *Cuadernos Hispanoamericanos*, 610 (April 2001), p. 96.

32 *Macedonio Fernández/Jorge Luis Borges: Correspondencia*, p. 223.

33 César Fernández Moreno, 'Weary of Labyrinths: An Interview with Jorge Luis Borges', *Encounter* (April 1969), p. 5.

34 Vazques, *Borges*, p. 60.

35 Jorge Luis Borges, *El libro de arena* (Buenos Aires, 1975), p. 19.

3 Buenos Aires, the Avant-garde and Literary Friendships

1 Jorge Luis Borges, *The Aleph and Other Stories, 1933–1969*, Norman Thomas di Giovanni, trans. and ed. in collaboration with the author (New York, 1970), p. 224.

2 Jorge Luis Borges, *El tamaño de mi esperanza* (Barcelona, 1993), p. 132.

3 Jorge Luis Borges, *Obras completas* (Buenos Aires, 1974), p. 17.

4 Jorge Luis Borges, *Textos recobrados 1919–1929* (Buenos Aires, 1997), p. 162.

5 *Obras completas*, p. 32.

6 Juan Cruz, 'Mis libros: Jorge Luis Borges entrevistado', *Vuelta*, 106 (September 1985), p. 42.

7 *The Aleph*, p. 225.

8 Jorge Luis Borges, *Inquisiciones* (Buenos Aires, 1993), p. 163.

9 Ibid., p. 29.

10 Yvonne Bordelois, 'Borges y Güiraldes: Historia de una pasión porteña', *Cuadernos Hispanoamericanos*, 585 (March 1999), p. 41.

11 *Textos recobrados*, p. 97.

12 Carlos Cortínez, ed., *Borges the Poet* (Fayetteville, AR, 1986), p. 39.

13 Carlos García, ed., *Macedonio Fernández/Jorge Luis Borges: Correspondencia 1922–1939. Crónica de una amistad* (Buenos Aires, 2000), p. 39.

14 *Textos recobrados*, p. 131.

15 *The Aleph*, p. 227.

16 *Macedonio Fernández/Jorge Luis Borges: Correspondencia*, p. 15.

17 Ibid., p. 180.

18 Ibid., p. 230.

19 María Esther Vázquez, *Borges: Esplendor y derrota* (Barcelona, 1996), p. 76.

20 César Fernández Moreno, 'Weary of Labyrinths: An Interview with Jorge Luis Borges', *Encounter* (April 1969), p. 8.

21 Juan Gustavo Cobo Borda, compilador, *El Aleph borgiano* (Bogotá,

1987), p. 68.

22 Jorge Luis Borges, Canning House, 'The Spanish Language in South America – A Literary Problem' / 'El gaucho Martín Fierro' (London, 1964), p. 10.

23 *Macedonio Fernández/Jorge Luis Borges: Correspondencia*, p. 263.

24 Ibid., p. 91.

25 Fernando Sorrentino, *Siete conversaciones con Jorge Luis Borges* [1972] (Buenos Aires, 2001), p. 180.

26 *Textos recobrados*, p. 318.

27 Carlos Mastronardi, *Memorias de un provinciano* (Buenos Aires, 1967), pp. 206–7.

28 María Teresa Gramuglio, 'El Borges de Mastronardi: Fragmentos de un autorretrato indirecto', *Cuadernos Hispanoamericanos*, 661–2 (July–August 2005), p. 67.

29 Willis Barnstone, *With Borges on an Ordinary Evening in Buenos Aires* (Urbana, IL, 1993), p. 3.

30 Ibid., p. 13.

31 Mastronardi, *Memorias*, p. 210.

32 Emir Rodríguez Monegal, *Jorge Luis Borges: A Literary Biography* (New York, 1978), p. 2.

33 Jorge Luis Borges and Ernesto Sábato, *Diálogos* (Buenos Aires, 1976), p. 54.

34 Alvaro Abós, *Xul Solar. Pintor del misterio* (Buenos Aires, 2004), p. 183. See also Patricia M. Artundo, ed., *Xul Solar: Entrevistas, artículos y textos inéditos* (Buenos Aires, 2005).

35 Ibid., p. 237.

36 Jorge Luis Borges, *Atlas*, trans. and annotated in collaboration with María Kodama and Anthony Kerrigan (New York, 1986), pp. 77–81.

37 Sorrentino, *Siete conversaciones*, p. 111.   cf note 25

38 Osvaldo Ferrari, *Borges en diálogo* (Buenos Aires, 1985), p. 184.

39 Ibid., p. 214.

40 *Borges en Sur, 1931–1999* (Buenos Aires, 1999), pp. 173–5.

41 *Macedonio Fernández/Jorge Luis Borges: Correspondencia*, p. 122.

42 Alberto Hidalgo, *De muertos, heridos y contusos* (San Isidro, 2004), pp. 19, 168.

43 *Textos recobrados*, pp. 349–50.

44 *Obras completas*, p. 857.

45 Jorge Luis Borges, *Oeuvres complètes*, 1, ed. Jean Pierre Bernès (Paris,

1993), p. 1313.

46 *Borges en Sur*, p. 62.

47 Ferrari, *Borges en diálogo*, pp. 153–5.   *fn 38*

48 *The Aleph*, p. 237.   *art?*

49 Miguel Capistrán, ed., *Borges y México* (México City, 1999), p. 99.   *?*

50 Ibid., pp. 120–21.   *^*

51 *El tamaño de mi esperanza*, p. 130.   *1926/43*

52 *The Aleph*, p. 237.

53 Jorge Schwartz, *Homenaje a Girondo* (Buenos Aires, 1987), p. 105.

54 Sorrentino, *Siete conversaciones*, p. 81.

55 Vázquez, *Borges*, p. 86.

56 Ramón Gómez de la Serna, 'Norah Borges', *La Gaceta*, 346 (October 1999), pp. 19–23.

57 María Angélica Bastos, *Borges y los otros* [1967] (Buenos Aires, 1999), pp. 48–9.

58 *Revista Martín Fierro 1924–1927*, facsimile edn (Buenos Aires, 1995), p. 332.

59 *Obras completas*, p. 42.

60 'Nota sobre el ultraismo', *Testigo*, 2 (April–June 1966), p. 9.

61 *Textos recobrados*, p. 397.

62 *The Aleph*, p. 237.

63 Ronald Christ, 'Jorge Luis Borges: An Interview', *Paris Review* (Winter/Spring 1967), p. 151.

4 The 1930s, Crisis and Accident

1 Jorge Luis Borges, *The Aleph and Other Stories, 1933–1969*, Norman Thomas di Giovanni, trans. and ed. in collaboration with the author (New York, 1970), p. 230.

2 Edwin Williamson, *Borges: A Life* (London, 2004), p. 163.

3 María Esther Vázquez, *Borges: Esplendor y derrota* (Barcelona, 1996), pp. 146–7.

4 Jorge Luis Borges, *Obras completas* (Buenos Aires, 1974), p. 842.

5 Ibid., pp. 95–6.

6 Donna J. Guy, *Sex and Danger in Buenos Aires: Prostitution, Family and Nation in Argentina* (Lincoln and London, 1990), p. 5.

7 María Esther de Miguel, *Norah Lange: Una biografía* (Buenos Aires,

1991), p. 31.

8 Julio Woscoboinik, *El secreto de Borges: Indagación psicoanalítica de su obra* (Buenos Aires, 1988), p. 117.

9 Emir Rodríguez Monegal, *Jorge Luis Borges: A Literary Biography* (New York, 1978), p. 349.

10 *Obras completas*, p. 862.

11 Fernando Sorrentino, *Siete conversaciones con Jorge Luis Borges* [1972] (Buenos Aires, 2001), p. 145.

12 *The Aleph*, p. 230.

13 Alex Zissman, 'An Interview with Jorge Luis Borges', *Cambridge Review*, 5 (May 1972), p. 111.

14 *Borges en El Hogar 1935–1958* (Buenos Aires, 2000), p. 167.

15 *Obras completas*, p. 289.

16 Ibid., p. 291.

17 Ibid., p. 291.

18 *The Aleph*, p. 238.

19 Vázquez, *Borges*, p. 52.

20 Luisa Valenzuela, 'El cuento olvidado de Borges', *La Nación* (22 August 1999), p. 60.

21 Fernando Sorrentino, *El Trujamán* (8 June 2005).
    www.cvc.cervantes.es/trujaman/anteriores/juno_05/08062005.htm

22 Ronald Christ, 'Jorge Luis Borges: An Interview', *Paris Review* (Winter/Spring 1967), p. 145.

23 'Homenaje a Jorge Luis Borges', *La Nación* (22 June 1986), p. 2.

24 *Obras completas*, p. 816.

25 *Borges en Sur, 1931–1999* (Buenos Aires, 1999), p. 63.

26 Jorge Luis Borges and Ernesto Sábato, *Diálogos* (Buenos Aires, 1976), p. 174.

27 *The Aleph*, p. 243.

28 Osvaldo Ferrari, *Borges en diálogo* (Buenos Aires, 1985), pp. 227–8 and *The Aleph*, pp. 240–43.

29 *Obras completas*, p. 406.

30 Ibid., p. 866.

31 Sorrentino, *Siete conversaciones*, p. 145.

32 'Especial Borges', *El País Cultural*, 85 (7 June 1991), p. 3.

33 Jorge Luis Borges, *Collected Fictions*, trans. Andrew Hurley (London, 1998), p. 175.

34 Arthur Schopenhauer, *Essays and Aphorisms*, trans. R. J. Hollingdale (Harmondsworth, 1970), p. 45.

35 Norman Thomas Di Giovanni, Frank MacShane and Daniel Halpern, eds, *Borges on Writing* (London, 1974), p. 58.

36 *Collected Fictions*, p. 178.

5 The 1940s, War, Peronism and Writing

1 Jorge Luis Borges, *The Aleph and Other Stories, 1933–1969*, Norman Thomas di Giovanni, trans. and ed. in collaboration with the author (New York, 1970), p. 241.

2 Jorge Luis Borges, *Oeuvres complètes*, 1, ed. Jean Pierre Bernès (Paris, 1993), p. 1556.

3 Luis Harss, 'Jorge Luis Borges o la consolación por la filosofía', *Los Nuestros* (Buenos Aires, 1966), p. 147.

4 Gustave Lanson, *Histoire Illustrée de la Littérature française*, II (Paris, 1923), p. 347.

5 *The Aleph*, p. 268.

6 Jorge Luis Borges, *Obras completas* (Buenos Aires, 1974), p. 488.

7 Harss, 'Jorge Luis Borges o la consolación por la filosofía', p. 152.

8 Horacio Salas, *Borges: Una biografía* (Buenos Aires, 1994), p. 205.

9 *Obras completas*, pp. 626–7.

10 Edwin Williamson, *Borges: A Life* (London, 2004), p. 409.

11 Borges, *Obras completas*, pp. 392–402.

12 Ibid., p. 629.

13 Edna Aizenberg, *Borges and his Successors: The Borgesian Impact on Literature and the Arts* (Columbia and London, 1990), pp. 127–41.

14 Jorge Luis Borges, *Textos recobrados 1919–1929* (Buenos Aires, 1997), pp. 89–90.

15 *Obras completas*, p. 727.

16 Ibid., p. 687.

17 *Borges en Sur, 1931–1999* (Buenos Aires, 1999), p. 304.

18 María Esther Vázquez, *Borges: Esplendor y derrota* (Barcelona, 1996), p. 22.

19 V. S. Naipaul, *The Return of Eva Peron* (London, 1980), p. 107.

20 *Obras completas*, p. 789.

21 Emir Rodríguez Monegal, *Jorge Luis Borges: A Literary Biography* (New York, 1978), p. 240.

p. 123 ʒ̸
140

22 Alberto Manguel, 'Borges in love', *Into the Looking Glass Wood* (London, 1999), p. 57.

23 Bernès, *Oeuvres complètes*, p. 1547.

24 Estela Canto, *Borges a contraluz* (Madrid, 1989), p. 83.

25 Vázquez, *Borges*, pp. 52–3.

26 Canto, *Borges a contraluz*, p. 143.

27 Norman Thomas Di Giovanni, Frank MacShane and Daniel Halpern, eds, *Borges on Writing* (London, 1974), p. 58.

28 Ernesto Sábato, *Tres aproximaciones a la literatura de nuestro tiempo* (Santiago, Chile, 1968), p. 47.

29 Juan José Sebreli, *Escritos sobre escritos, ciudades bajo ciudades, 1955–1997* (Buenos Aires, 1997), p. 466.

30 *Textos recobrados*, p. 148.

31 Christopher Isherwood, *The Condor and the Cows* (London, 1949), p. 192.

32 G. S. Fraser, *News from South America* (London, 1949), pp. 115–22.

6 From Blindness to Geneva

1 Jorge Luis Borges, *The Aleph and Other Stories, 1933–1969*, Norman Thomas di Giovanni, trans. and ed. in collaboration with the author (New York, 1970), p. 258.

2 J. M. Coetzee, 'Borges's Dark Mirror', *New York Review of Books* (22 October 1998), p. 81.

3 Michael Wood, 'Borges's Surprise!', *New York Review of Books* (1 June 1972), p. 32.

4 Edwin Williamson, *Borges: A Life* (London, 2004), p. 415.

5 Susan Sontag, *Where the Stress Falls* (London, 2002), p. 112.

6 'Homenaje a Jorge Luis Borges', *La Nación* (22 June 1986), p. 86.

7 *The Aleph*, p. 250.

8 Jorge Luis Borges, *Obras completas* (Buenos Aires, 1974), p. 809.

9 Ronald Christ, 'Jorge Luis Borges: An Interview', *Paris Review* (Winter/Spring 1967), p. 118.

10 *Obras completas*, p. 809.

11 Jorge Luis Borges, *Siete noches* (Buenos Aires, 1980), pp. 169–70.

12 *Obras completas*, p. 1098.

13 *The Aleph*, p. 254.

14 Jorge Luis Borges, *Nueve ensayos dantescos dantescos*, intro. Marcos Ricardo Barnatán (Madrid, 1982), p. 153.

15 Alan Pauls, *El factor Borges* (Barcelona, 2004).

16 V. S. Naipaul, *The Return of Eva Perón* (London, 1980), pp. 122–8.

17 Willis Barnstone, *With Borges on an Ordinary Evening in Buenos Aires* (Urbana, IL, 1993), p. 63. *p. 19 foto*

18 *Clarín*, 26 August 1982.

19 Alberto Manguel, 'Borges in Love', *Into the Looking Glass Wood* (London, 1999), p. 60.

20 See review of Borges's *Collected Fictions* in Jason Wilson, 'Life Member of the Gaucho Club', *The Independent Weekend Review*, 6 February 1999, p. 15.

21 *Clarín*, 10 August 1991.

22 Williamson, *Borges: A Life*, p. 488. *fn 4 p 132*

23 Carlos Cortínez, ed., *Borges the Poet* (Fayetteville, AR, 1986), p. 57.

24 *Obras completas*, p. 858.

25 Ibid., p. 771.

26 Enrique Pezzoni, 'Fervor de Buenos Aires: Autobiografía y autorretrato', *El texto y sus voces* (Buenos Aires, 1986), p. 75.

27 *Obras completas*, p. 937.

28 Ibid., p. 975.

29 Emir Rodríguez Monegal, *Jorge Luis Borges: A Literary Biography* (New York, 1978), p. 240.

30 Paul Theroux, *The Old Patagonian Express: By Train through the Americas* (Harmondsworth, 1980), p. 399.

31 Willis Barnstone, *Borges at Eighty: Conversations* (Bloomington, IN, 1982), p. 35.

32 *Jorge Luis Borges: A Literary Biography*, p. 466.

Needed is a list of Borges'
    books in chronological order

Bibliography

Editions

I have used the last complete works that Jorge Luis Borges prepared himself in Spanish, his *Obras completas* (Buenos Aires, 1974). I have consulted the magnificent annotated edition in French that he also approved of, the *Oeuvres complètes*, 1, ed. Jean Pierre Bernès (Paris, 1993). The English translations used are the latest, *Collected Fictions*, trans. Andrew Hurley (London, 1998), though I have translated the poetry quoted myself in a literal way. I have also cited from Borges's memoirs in English in *The Aleph and Other Stories 1933–1969: together with Commentaries and an Autobiographical Essay*, ed. and trans. by Norman Thomas di Giovanni in collaboration with the author (New York, 1970).

Further editions of Borges's works used

'The Spanish Language in South America – a Literary Problem' /
    'El gaucho Martín Fierro' (London, 1964)
'Nota sobre el ultraismo', *Testigo*, 2 (April–June 1966), pp. 8–9
El libro de arena (Buenos Aires, 1975)
Prólogos (Buenos Aires, 1975)
Norah (Milan, 1977)
Obras completas en colaboración (Buenos Aires, 1979)
Siete noches (Buenos Aires, 1980)
La cifra (Madrid, 1981)
Nueve ensayos dantescos, intro. Marcos Ricardo Barnatán
    (Madrid, 1982)

Textos cautivos: Ensayos y reseñas en 'El Hogar' (1936–1939) (Barcelona, 1986)
Atlas, in collaboration with María Kodama, trans. Anthony Kerrigan (New York, 1986)
El Aleph borgiano, ed. Juan Gustavo Cobo Borda, (Bogotá, 1987)
El tamaño de mi esperanza (Barcelona, 1993 [1926])
Inquisiciones (Buenos Aires, 1993 [1925])
Siete noches (Buenos Aires, 1997)
Textos recobrados 1919–1929 (Buenos Aires, 1997)
El idioma de los argentinos (Madrid, 1998 [1928])
Cartas del fervor: Correspondencia con Maurice Abramowicz y Jacobo Sureda (1919–1928), prologue Joaquín Marco (Barcelona, 1999)
Borges en Sur, 1931–1980 (Buenos Aires, 1999)
Selected Poems, ed. Alexander Coleman, trans. W. S. Merwin, et al. (London, 1999)
The Total Library: Non-Fiction, 1922–1986, ed. Eliot Weinberger, trans. Esther Allen, Suzanne Jill Levine and Eliot Weinberger (London, 2000)
Borges en El Hogar 1935–1958 (Buenos Aires, 2000)
Macedonio Fernández/Jorge Luis Borges: Correspondencia: 1922–1939. Crónica de una amistad, Carlos García, ed. (Buenos Aires, 2000)
El Aleph de Jorge Luis Borges, facsimile edn, ed. Julio Ortega and Elena del Río Parra (México, 2001)
Textos recobrados, 1931–1955 (Buenos Aires, 2002)
El círculo secreto: Prólogos y notas (Buenos Aires, 2003)

Biographies

Barnatán, Marcos Ricardo, *Borges: Biografía total* (Madrid, 1995)
Barnstone, Willis, *With Borges on an Ordinary Evening in Buenos Aires* (Urbana, IL, 1993) ✓ p. 19 (foto) p. 140
Bastos, María Angélica, *Borges y los otros* (Buenos Aires, 1999 [1967])
Canto, Estela, *Borges a contraluz* (Madrid, 1989)
Rodríguez Monegal, Emir, *Borgès par lui-même* (Paris, 1970)
——, *Jorge Luis Borges: A Literary Biography* (New York, 1978)
Salas, Horacio, *Borges: Una biografía* (Buenos Aires, 1994)
Teitelboim, Volodia, *Los dos Borges: vida, sueños, enigmas* (Santiago de Chile, 1996)

p 23

Torre Borges, Miguel de, *Borges: Fotografías y manuscritos* (Buenos Aires, 1987)

Uveda de Robledo, Epifanía and Alejandro Vaccaro, *El señor Borges* (Buenos Aires, 2004)

Vaccaro, Alejandro, *Georgie (1899–1930): Una vida de Jorge Luis Borges* (Buenos Aires, 1996)

Vázquez, María Esther, *Borges. Esplendor y derrota* (Barcelona, 1996)

Williamson, Edwin, *Borges: A Life* (London, 2004)

Woodall, James, *The Man in the Mirror of the Book: A Life of Jorge Luis Borges* (London, 1996)

Interviews

Barnstone, Willis, *Borges at Eighty: Conversations* (Bloomington, IN, 1982)

Boncenne, Pierre, 'Jorge Luis Borges s'explique', *Magazine Lire* (September 1980), pp. 31–43

Borges, Jorge Luis and Ernesto Sábato, *Diálogos* (Buenos Aires, 1976)

Chao, Ramón and Ignacio Ramonet, 'Entretien avec Jorge Luis Borges', *Le Monde* (19 April 1978), p. 2

Charbonnier, Georges, *Entretiens avec Jorge Luis Borges* (Paris, 1967)

Christ, Ronald, 'Jorge Luis Borges: An Interview', *Paris Review* (Winter/Spring 1967), pp. 116–64

Cruz, Jorge, 'Mis libros: Jorge Luis Borges entrevistado', *Vuelta*, 106 (September 1985), pp. 40–6

Di Giovanni, Norman Thomas, Frank MacShane and Daniel Halpern, eds, *Borges on Writing* (London, 1974)

Fernández Moreno, César, 'Weary of Labyrinths: An Interview with Jorge Luis Borges', *Encounter* (April 1969), pp. 3–14

Ferrari, Osvaldo, *Borges en diálogo* (Buenos Aires, 1985)

Harss, Luis, 'Jorge Luis Borges o la consolación por la filosofía', *Los Nuestros* (Buenos Aires, 1966)

Pivot, Bernard, 'Borges oral', *La Jornada Semanal* (23 March 1997)

Sorrentino, Fernando, *Siete conversaciones con Jorge Luis Borges* (Buenos Aires, 2001)

Spurling, John, 'The Argentinian Writer Jorge Luis Borges', *The Listener* (8 July 1971), pp. 41–4

Vázquez, María Esther, *Borges, sus días y su tiempo* (Buenos Aires, 1984)
Zissman, Alex, 'An Interview with Jorge Luis Borges', *Cambridge Review*, 5
    (May 1972), pp. 108–18

Bibliographies and index

Balderston, Daniel, *The Literary Universe of Jorge Luis Borges: An Index to
    References and Allusions to persons, Titles, and Places in his Writings*
    (New York, 1986)
Becco, Horacio Jorge, *Jorge Luis Borges: Bibliografía total, 1923–1973*
    (Buenos Aires, 1973)
Helft, Nicolás, *Jorge Luis Borges: Bibliografía completa*, prologue Noé
    Jitrik (Buenos Aires, 1997)
Jorge Luis Borges (1899–1986) (London, 2003)
Lowenstein, Javed, *A Descriptive Catalogue of the Jorge Luis Borges
    Collection at the University of Virginia* (Charlottesville, VA, 1993)
Bibliography at the Borges Center, The University of Iowa,
    www.uiowa.edu/borges

Books

Abós, Alvaro, *Xul Solar: Pintor del misterio* (Buenos Aires, 2004)
Aizenberg, Edna, ed., *Borges and his Successors: The Borgesian Impact on
    Literature and the Arts* (Columbia and London, 1990)
——, *Books and Bombs in Buenos Aires: Borges, Gerchunoff, and
    Argentine-Jewish Writing* (Hanover and London, 2002)
Artudo, Patricia M., ed., *Xul Solar: Entrevistas, artículos y textas inéditos*
    (Buenos Aires, 2005)
Ayerza de Castillo, Laura and Odile Felgine, *Victoria Ocampo* (Barcelona, 1993)
Bernés, Jean-Pierre, *Album Jorge Luis Borges* (Paris, 1999)
Bloom, Harold, *The Western Canon. The Books and School of the Ages*
    (London, 1995)
Capistrán, Miguel, ed., *Borges y México* (México City, 1999)
Cortínez, Carlos, ed., *Borges the Poet* (Fayetteville, AR, 1986)
Di Giovanni, Norman Thomas, *The Lesson of the Master: On Borges and his*

Work (London, 2003)

Fishburn, Evelyn and Psiche Hughes, eds, *A Dictionary of Borges* (London, 1990)

Fishburn, Evelyn, ed., *Borges and Europe Revisted* (London, 1998)

Fló, Juan, ed., *Contra Borges* (Buenos Aires, 1978)

Fraser, G. S., *News from South America* (London, 1949)

Gombrowicz, Witold, *Diario argentino* (Buenos Aires, 1968)

Guy, Donna J., *Sex and Danger in Buenos Aires: Prostitution, Family, and Nation in Argentina* (Lincoln and London, 1990)

Hidalgo, Alberto, *De muertos, heridos y contusos* (San Isidro, 2004)

Isherwood, Christopher, *The Condor and the Cows* (London, 1949)

Jurado, A., *El mundo de la palabra: Memorias 1952–1972* (Buenos Aires, 1990)

King, John, *Sur: A Study of the Argentine Literary Journal and its role in the Development of a Culture, 1931–1970* (Cambridge, 1986)

Manguel, Alberto, 'Borges in love', *Into the Looking Glass Wood* (London, 1999) *cf p. 173 & 140 above*

Martínez, Tomás Eloy, *El sueño argentino* (Buenos Aires, 1999)

Mastronardi, Carlos, *Memorias de un provinciano* (Buenos Aires, 1967)

Michaux, Henri, *Oeuvres complètes*, 1, ed. Raymond Bellow (Paris, 1998)

Miguel, María Esther de, *Norah Lange: Una biografía* (Buenos Aires, 1991)

Naipaul, V. S., *The Return of Eva Perón* (London, 1980)

Ocampo, Victoria and Roger Caillois, *Correspondencia (1939–1978)*, ed. Odile Felgine (Buenos Aires, 1999)

Pauls, Alan, *El factor Borges* (Barcelona, 2004)

Pezzoni, Enrique, 'Fervor de Buenos Aires. autobiografía y autorretrato', *El texto y sus voces* (Buenos Aires, 1986)

Revista Martín Fierro 1924–1927, facsimile edn (Buenos Aires, 1995)

Sábato, Ernesto, *Tres aproximaciones a la literature de nuestro tiempo* (Santiago, Chile, 1968)

Sarlo, Beatriz, *La pasión y la excepción* (Buenos Aires, 2003)

Schwartz, Jorge, *Homenaje a Girondo* (Buenos Aires, 1987)

Sebreli, Juan José, *Escritos sobre escritos, ciudades bajo ciudades, 1950–1997* (Buenos Aires, 1997)

Sontag, Susan, *Where the Stress Falls* (London, 2002)

Theroux, Paul, *The Old Patagonian Express: By Train through the Americas* (Harmondsworth, 1980)

Woscoboinik, Julio, *El secreto de Borges: Indagación psicoanalítica de su Obra* (Buenos Aires, 1988)

Zito, Carlos Alberto, *El Buenos Aires de Borges* (Buenos Aires, 1998)

Articles

Anzieu, Didier, 'Psicoanálisis de Borges', *La Opinión* (19 September 1971), pp. 1–3

Baur, Sergio, 'Norah Borges, musa de las vanguardias', *Cuadernos Hispanoamericanos*, 610 (April 2001)

Bell-Villada, Gene H., 'Borges as Argentine Author, and Other Self-Evident (if Often Ignored) Truths', *Salmagundi*, 82–83 (Spring/Summer 1989), pp. 305–19

Bernès, Jean-Pierre, 'Borges o el viejo anarquista apacible', interview with Gérard de Cortanze, *La Gaceta* (October 1999), pp. 19–23

Bianciotti, Héctor, 'Le bibliothécaire de Babel', *Le Monde* (17 June 1986), pp. 1, 16

Bordelois, Yvonne, 'Borges y Güiraldes: historia de una pasión porteña', *Cuadernos Hispanoamericanos*, 585 (March 1999), pp. 7–18

Castello, Cristina,'Entrevista con María Kodama', *Cuadernos Hispanoamericanos*, 651–2 (September–October 2004), pp. 219–30

Coetzee, J. M., 'Borges's Dark Mirror', *New York Review of Books* (22 October 1998), pp. 80–2

'Especial Borges', *El País Cultural*, 85 (7 June 1991), pp. 1–20

Gómez de la Serna, Ramón, 'Norah Borges', *La Gaceta*, 346 (October 1999), pp. 39–44

Gramuglio, María Teresa, 'El Borges de Mastronardi: Fragmentos de un autorretrato indirecto', *Cuadernos Hispanoamericanos*, 661–2 (July–August 2005), pp. 63–76

Graves, Robert, 'Borges, Banshees and Basilisks', *New Statesman* (27 November 1970), pp. 716–18

'Homenaje a Jorge Luis Borges', *La Nación* (22 June 1986), pp. 1–8

Lafon, Michel, 'Algunos ejercicios de escritura en colaboración' in Sylvia Saíta, ed., *El oficio se afirma*, *Historia de la literatura argentina*, 9 (Emecé, 2004), pp. 65–90

Pacheco, José Emilio, 'En los abismos de "El Aleph"', *Letras Libres* (January 2003), pp. 26–8

Valenzuela, Luisa, 'El cuento olvidado de Borges', *La Nación* (22 August 1999), pp. 59–69

Wilson, Jason, 'Borges and Buenos Aires (and Brothels)', *Donaire* (13 December 1999), pp. 47–54

—— , 'Jorge Luis Borges and the European Avant-Garde' in Evelyn
    Fishburn, ed., *Borges and Europe Revisted* (London, 1998)
—— , 'The Mutating City: Buenos Aires and the Avant-garde: Borges, Xul
    Solar, and Marechal' in *Hispanic Research Journal*, IV/3 (October 2003),
    pp. 251–69
Wood, Michael, 'Borges's Surprise!', *New York Review of Books* (1 June
    1972), pp. 32–3

Acknowledgements

I would like to thank many people who, often unwittingly, have contributed to this book with cuttings, advice, often through chatting. I merely list names: Humberto Núñez, Evie Fishburn, Edwin Williamson, Patricia Novillo, Nick Caistor, Norman Thomas di Giovanni, José Viñals, Ricardo Ferrera, Fernando Sorrentino, Eduardo Berti, Anthony Edkins, Willis Barnstone, Roland-François Lack, Alejandro Manara, Vivian Constantinopoulos (and all the staff at Reaktion Books) and especially Andrea, who combed the text, and Camila, who helped with the photos.